they'd none
of 'em
be
missed

KK

RICHARD SUART AND A. S. H. SMYTH

THEY'D NONE OF 'EM BE MISSED

CONTENTS

Opposite: 'Why, I love her myself. Charming little girl, isn't she?' – a scene from the 1938 film with Martyn Green as Ko-Ko and Kenny Baker as Nanki-Poo

FOREWORD BY JONATHAN MILLER

One of the great pleasures of working in opera as opposed to the theatre is the fact that, if you are lucky, the production is revived several times after its première, and although the cast is often completely different on each of the subsequent performances, from time to time some of the principals return and virtually take possession of a particular role, so that after a while it's difficult to visualize the production without their distinctive performance.

I don't think that any of us imagined that the ENO production of *The Mikado* would come back again and again more than twenty years after its first performance, and I doubt if Richard Suart foresaw his many re-appearances as Ko-Ko. By now however his portrayal of the Lord High Executioner has become a legendary part of our production and you can tell from their reaction that the audience revels in his idiosyncratic version of this cocky opportunist. Added to which they gasp, sometimes with shocked disbelief at the inventive irreverence of his repeatedly re-invented Little List. So it's a great delight to have a complete anthology of Richard's rhymic ribaldries from which the reader can appreciate the social and political idiocies of two decades. Bravissimo!

Tokyo, Winter 2007

Opposite: with Richard Van Allan as Pooh-Bah and Eric Shilling as Pish-Tush

SAVOY THEATRE
THE MIKADO
R. D'OYLY CARTE. Proprietor and Manager.

INTRODUCTION

The Mikado, Gilbert and Sullivan's ninth operatic collaboration, opened to critical and public acclaim at the Savoy Theatre on 14th March 1885. With numbers including *Three little maids*, *Tit-willow*, and *A wand'ring minstrel*, and characters such as the love-lorn hero Nanki-Poo and the gorgeous Yum-Yum, it is still one of our best loved comic operas.

But it is the hapless anti-hero Ko-Ko, Lord High Executioner of Titipu, whom we remember in this book, and specifically his celebrated Little List.

> Gentlemen, I'm much touched by this reception. I can only trust that by strict attention to duty I shall ensure a continuance of those favours which it will ever be my study to deserve. If I should ever be called upon to act professionally, I am happy to think that there will be no difficulty in finding plenty of people whose loss will be a distinct gain to society at large.

Not a bad opening speech for an ex-tailor who had been condemned to death for flirting, but who had been reprieved at the last moment, a sudden change of fortune owed entirely to the legislative urges of the Mikado who had most recently (and most unambiguously) decreed that whoever

> Flirted, leered or winked
> (Unless connubially linked),
> Should forthwith be beheaded.

Opposite: Cover for the original programme distributed to patrons in the more expensive seats

MR. GROSSMITH IN "THE MIKADO."
COPYRIGHT
Barraud 263 Oxford St London
A few doors West of The Circus.

George Grossmith as Ko-Ko, the role he created in 1885

Unhappy with the decree, fellow Titipudlians hit upon the ingenious notion of voting the next on death row to become Headsman, reasoning that

> Who's next to be decapited
> Cannot cut off another's head
> Until he's cut his own off.

And so, by Gilbertian twist and turn, Ko-Ko's list of offenders was born – a catalogue of irritants (other than Ko-Ko himself, naturally) of whom society might well be rid. Gilbert was, in many regards, one of the original Grumpy Old Men; and while his Little List presents us with some stereotypically tiresome features of late-Victorian English life, there is no doubt that all who were included in the original were the personal pet hates of the irascible humorist.

Gilbert not only wrote the libretti for his collaborations with Sullivan, but also directed the operas. He ran a tyrannical regime at the Savoy that allowed little individuality in the playing of the roles; if an artist did not adhere to his wishes, or faltered from his direction, draconian fines were imposed. That a singer might tamper with his text was in the circumstances absolutely unthinkable.

And thus the sanctity of Gilbert's libretto was (more or less) respected for the next seven decades. But that didn't stop interpreters of the role 'updating' the text by alluding to present-day politicians through mime. George Grossmith, the creator of the role, impersonated Gladstone,

Salisbury and even Joseph Chamberlain; Sir Henry Lytton, who sang the role over a period of twenty-six years (1908-1934) was a dab hand at Lloyd George and Stanley Baldwin.

John Reed also entered into the realms of political impersonation, with Wilson and Heath. Gilbert's third verse was the moment to watch out for this:

> … apologetic statesmen of a compromising kind,
> Such as – what d'ye call him – Thing'em bob, and likewise
> Never Mind,
> And 'St – 'st – 'st – and What's-his-name, and also You-know-who…

But it was in 1985 that we first had a new Little List in London. *The Metropolitan Mikado* at the Queen Elizabeth Hall was adapted by Ned Sherrin and Alistair Beaton. Ko-Ko became Chief Police Commissioner of Mitsubishi, a character noted for his tough approach, small feet and enormous ears. His Little List included:

> The immigrant who visits us and stays here far too long,
> And people who read Guardians and live in Islington.

The following year Jonathan Miller's 1930s-style production of *The Mikado* made its debut at the Coliseum for English National Opera. Eric Idle sang the part of Ko-Ko, with a completely rewritten Little List as his tour de force.

Henry Lytton, 1924

Eric Idle as Ko-Ko at ENO, 1986

> There's interior designers, window dressers and that sort,
> Bank robbers who retire to Spain the minute they get caught.
> And nasty little editors whose papers are the pits,
> They fill their rags with gossip and with huge and floppy… writs.

He also nicely reworked Gilbert's original political lines in verse three to include

> … modern politicians of the image-making kind
> Such as Mrs. Thing, and Doctor – oh – and likewise… never mind.

Almost overnight, Idle created a new Gilbert and Sullivan tradition. No longer do audiences crave for the 'Here's a how-de-do' encores; now everyone wants to hear which scurrilous major (and not-so-major) celebrities have made it to the finishing post. Which brings us, inevitably, to the book you now have in your hands, written jointly by the performer and his much younger assistant. The one provides the inspiration, and the other the discipline and readability.

At the Coliseum (still performing the now-famous Miller production), the Little List is delivered with the aid of a microphone and in the manner of a soap-box oration – in other words, it is read and not memorised, and changes can be made at will. The day's text is placed by me in my jacket pocket just after the overture; but I first enter in tennis whites, the jacket only being put on, in great haste, after 'Taken from the county jail.' In this I am ably assisted by two dressers – off go the shorts, on go the trousers and jacket in a matter of seconds – and I must confess that I live in fear of those lines vanishing. Accordingly – and with all due respect to the ENO's stage assistants – at the beginning of the show I stick a copy down my underpants, just in case. Mercifully, I have never had recourse to use my back-up… so far…

Inspiration for new lines comes from many sources – not just current affairs as described in the media, but also quirky turns of fate – for instance a photo of Johnny Wilkinson:

> These lyrics aren't by Gilbert, not by any means at all,
> He's been busy autographing every Rugby World Cup ball.

Well, that's one way I can justify re-writes – and I tend to leave the odd pair of lines right up to the last moment in the hopes of that blinding flash of light… Away from the Coliseum, a trip to Cromer one blustery Sunday night for a G&S concert on the Pier, where you could actually feel the structure moving, prompted:

> Lord Lucan has been missing now for many a livelong year,
> But in Cromer we've the answer to the disappearing pier.

Shortly before a visit to Fakenham in Norfolk, the delightful market

Taken from the county jail

town had been voted one of the most boring places in England to live – I begged to differ:

> The best time to eat fresh rolls is just soon after they've been
> bakin' 'em,
> It might not lead to orgasm, but at least there's no more
> Fakenham.

Incidentally, for readers who have concerns in this department, Ko-Ko can recommend;

> … that oval, blue, expensive pill is high upon the list,
> Yes, Viagra's on my list, one a day must not be missed.

In reviewing the Little Lists this particular Ko-Ko has had the honour to compile since 1988, I note that some minor irritants occur with alarming regularity. While it is interesting in its own way to note the same names (or types) cropping up time after time, to avoid this kind of repetition I have chosen not to provide whole Little Lists by date, but rather to list the offenders according to category. Though this means that chronological order is not strictly observed, it is for the most part maintained by default.

This modest offering, of course, does not set out to deal comprehensively with parodies and updates of the Little List – but I have reprinted, with permission, a few that others have written; they are a rich sample of even richer pickings.

HILDESHEIMER & FAULKNER, LONDON E.C.
DESIGNED IN ENGLAND
GEO. C. WHITNEY, NEW-YORK.
PRINTED IN GERA

Before we get going, here is a gem. I am most grateful to Peter Joslin for permission to reprint the following charming booklet which comes from his wide-ranging collection of memorabilia: he writes…

The Mikado *has proved a rich source for souvenirs. These include several fans, a Birthday Book, a bisque model of the three little maids as well as the usual crop of American trade cards of the main characters in the opera. However the production of a little booklet with the title* People who never would be missed *is probably unique. There is no publication date and the name of the author of the words is not mentioned, although the artist Henry Reynolds is. We do not know if Gilbert had anything to do with the production and if not why he did not make a fuss about it being issued with no acknowledgement to him. Only a very few copies seem to have survived. One is mentioned in the Pierpont Morgan Library's (New York) booklet* The Mikado A Centenary Celebration *(1985). The fact that it was produced by Hildescheimer & Faulkner and printed in Germany indicates that the booklet was a quality item. Hildescheimer & Faulkner were responsible for the better class programmes that were given to those in the best seats at the Savoy Theatre. Richard D'Oyly Carte employed them to supply these programmes for the theatre. Was he responsible for the booklet? Would he have risked Gilbert's ire, or was Gilbert complicit?*

The copy reproduced here was acquired many years ago and where it was found has long been forgotten. One page was used by Nicholas John when he edited the ENO programme for the first performances of Jonathan Miller's production of The Mikado *in 1986.*

AN ILLUSTRATED
SONG
OF PEOPLE WHO NEVER
WOULD BE MISSED.
PICTURED BY
Henry Reynolds.
HILDESHEIMER & FAULKNER
LONDON, E.C.

As some day it may happen that a victim must be found,
I've got a little list—I've got a little list
Of social offenders who might well be underground,
And who never would be missed—who never would be missed!
There's the pestilential nuisances
who write for
Autographs—
All people who have flabby hands
and irritating laughs—

All children who are up in dates, and floor you with 'em flat—
All persons who in shaking hands,
shake hands with you like *that*—
And all third persons who on
spoiling *tête-à-tetes* insist—
They'd none of be missed—
they'd none of 'em be missed!
Chorus.
He's got 'em on the list— he's got
'em on the list;
And they'll none of 'em be missed—They'll none of 'em be missed.

There's the nigger serenader, and the others of his race,
And the piano organist—I've got him on the list!
And the people who eat pepp'rmint and puff it in your face,

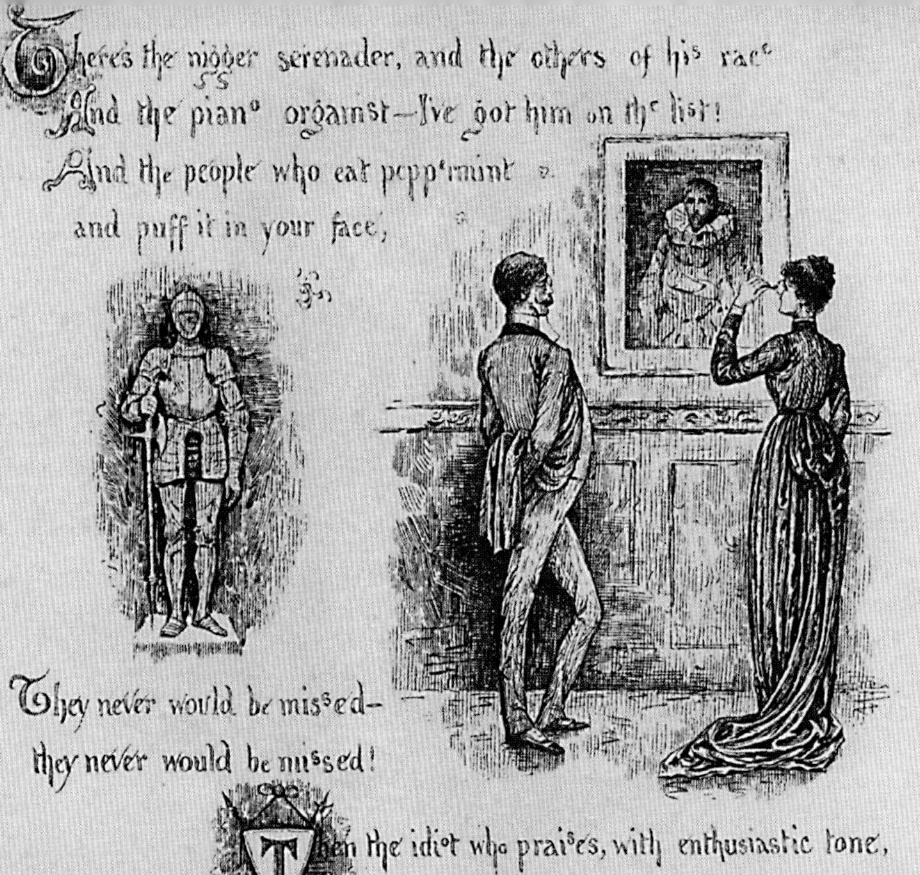

They never would be missed—
they never would be missed!

Then the idiot who praises, with enthusiastic tone,
All centuries but this, and every country but his own;

And that *Nisi Prius* nuisance, who just now is rather rife,
The Judicial humorist — I've got *him* on the list!

All funny fellows, comic men, and clowns of private life —
They'd none of 'em be missed — they'd none of 'em be missed

And apologetic statesmen of a compromising kind,
Such as—what d'ye call him—Thing'em bob,
and likewise Never Mind,
And 'St—'st—'st—and
What's-his-name, and
also You-know-who—
The task of filling
up the blanks I'd
rather leave to *you*.

But it really does'nt matter whom you put upon the list.
For they'd none of 'em be missed—they'd none of 'em be missed!

CHORUS

You may put 'em on the list—you may put 'em on the list,
And they'll none of 'em be missed—they'll none of 'em be missed!

As I have mentioned, the onus on earlier Ko-Kos was to illustrate the various politicians in the last verse. Martyn Green wrote in his Treasury of Gilbert and Sullivan*: 'As a general rule, mimed business was used to point to certain statesmen. In spite of Gilbert's stopping short of mentioning actual names – there is little doubt that he directed this mimed business.' Joseph Chamberlain would be indicated by inserting a monocle in the eye – and in later years Neville Chamberlain was suggested by opening, in mime, an umbrella. Lloyd George was invoked by making a golf stroke. 'Occasionally I was taken to task by people who wrote deploring the "insult" to great men. My experience has been that those who were so "insulted" never took it in any other way than that in which it was intended – a spirit of good fun.'*

The D'Oyly Carte London season of 1951 opened at the Savoy with The Mikado. *Churchill (whose moustachioed father we see opposite, with Lloyd George and Gladstone) was present on the first night, and sat in the Royal Box. At the time he was not Prime Minister but merely Leader of the Opposition, and a General Election was looming. Martyn continues: 'As I made my entrance as Ko-Ko, I knew that I had some very pointed words to sing. I also knew that on no account should I look in his direction, unless I could find the right moment. Up to the point of half-way through the last verse, I had not found the moment in my mind,'*

> And apologetic statesmen of a compromising kind *(gusts of laughter)*
> Such as – What d'ye call him – Thing'em-bob, and likewise – Never mind *(shrieks)*
> And 'ST – 'st-'st – and What's-his-name, and also You-know-who –

And yes, at this moment he found his eyes veering to the Royal Box, and yes, he brought the house down.

GILBERT'S ORIGINAL LITTLE LIST

Various aspects of the Little List were subject to change even under Gilbert's watchful eye, not least the position of the song in the opera. At the first performances, Ko-Ko sang his Little List much later in Act One: in fact it came as a response to a letter, handed to him by Pish-Tush. This reads:

> The Mikado is struck by the fact that no executions have taken place in Titipu for a year, and decrees that unless somebody is beheaded within one month, the post of Lord High Executioner shall be abolished, and the city reduced to the rank of a village.
>
> Pish-Tush: But that will involve us all in irretrievable ruin!
>
> Ko-Ko: Yes – somebody will have to suffer. Send the Recorder to me. (Exit P-T).
>
> I expected something of this sort! I knew it couldn't go on! Well, they've brought it on themselves, and the only question is, Who shall it be? Fortunately, there will be no difficulty in pitching upon somebody whose death will be a distinct gain to society.
>
> As it seems to be essential that a victim should be found,
> I've got a little list – I've got a little list
> Of social offenders who might well be underground,
> And who never would be missed – who never would be missed!

Opposite: Gilbert in his study at Grim's Dyke 1911

There's the pestilential nuisances who write for autographs –
All people who have flabby hands and irritating laughs –
All children who are up in dates, and floor you with 'em flat –
All persons who in shaking hands, shake hands with you like *that*
And all third persons who on spoiling *tête-à-têtes* insist –
They'd none of 'em be missed – they'd none of 'em be missed!
As a victim must be found,
If you'll only look around,
There are criminals at large,
(And enough to fill a barge),
Whose swift decapitation
Would be hailed with acclamation,
If accomplished by the nation
At a reasonable charge.

The second and third verses follow the text shown in the illustrated pamphlet reproduced above; those of you familiar with what we have come to know as the Little List will note some changes in the first few lines (and in the preamble), but otherwise most of this survived the move to earlier in the act, just after Ko-Ko's entrance. What is most interesting, dramatically, about the original version is that Ko-Ko must have been alone on stage when he sang this; it is clear that no chorus was present. The altered refrains, therefore, were sung by Ko-Ko alone – I think I regret

Opposite: Martyn Green, Henry Lytton's successor, in the 1938 film

Peter Pratt, who succeeded Martyn Green in 1951

their demise! Nevertheless, the song was moved to its current position after only a few nights.

Though most Ko-Kos were incredibly circumspect about making adjustments to Gilbert's words, under exceptional circumstances changes did creep in. In the 1920s Sir Henry Lytton included 'the prohibitionist', and in the Second World War, that singular anomaly became 'the clothing rationist'.

In other circumstances, though, alterations were made for less stylistic reasons. The 'nigger serenader' of the second verse lasted until 1948, at which point A. P. Herbert was called upon to find a substitute phrase, since when the 'banjo serenader' has been used. The change was announced in a rather official way by Rupert D'Oyly Carte in a letter to *The Times* on 28 May:

> We found recently in America that much objection was taken by coloured persons to a word used twice in *The Mikado* [it also appeared in the Mikado's song], a word which I shall not quote but which your readers may easily guess. Many protests and letters were received, and we consulted the witty writer on whose shoulders the lyrical mantle of Gilbert may be said to have fallen. He made several suggestions, one of which we adopted in America, and it seems well to continue doing so in the British Empire. Gilbert would surely have approved, and the alteration will be heard during our season at Sadler's Wells.

It is telling that D'Oyly Carte felt obliged to announce the matter in this way. Quite apart from the obvious implication that racist terms were still in common usage – at least in 'The British Empire' where it would seem no-one minded (no-one white, anyway) – the fact of broadcasting such a change in a major national paper indicates an interesting assumption (probably correct) regarding the social standing of this one song and, by extension, of *The Mikado* as a whole. We might conclude that Gilbert had a right to be jealous of every last detail of his work; it is hard to imagine a comparably important cultural work embraced by the establishment of 2008.

Does this mean that the lines are sacrosanct? Perhaps, and perhaps not. Many purists believe that no-one should ever be allowed to interfere with the 'original' text – that which Gilbert hath joined together, etc. – but plenty of other changes were made from the outset by Gilbert himself (and probably, bravely, by others rather more lowly). An early prompt copy sees several crossings-out and new additions. The 'lady novelist' soon became the 'critic dramatist'; or

> That source of grave predicament, the scorching bicyclist/motorist

Or

> That public curse, the frothy Hyde Park elocutionist.

Other new lines help us with the history (and the broad-mindedness!) of the day:

John Reed, who succeeded Peter Pratt in 1959

… that cruel but comic coward, the depraved John Chinaman,
We've taught him all the lessons that a single nation can.
But if Europe were agreed the malefactor's neck to twist
I don't think he'd be missed – I don't think he'd be missed.

The licence copy contains an early re-write of the later lines of the first verse, which also appears in the full score published in 1898 in Leipzig.

There's the Income Tax Commissioners with all their prying
clerks
And vulgar little streetboys who are rude in their remarks,
All persons with presentiments, a very wholesome rule,
And next-door neighbours everywhere, and boys at home from
school,
All men who bite their nails, all people who revoke at whist,
They'd none of 'em be missed – they'd none of 'em be missed.

Gilbert even added a whole new verse for the 1908 revival, to be used as an encore:

That well intentioned lady who's too bulky for her boots,
The lovely suffragist – I've got her on the list.
That single-minded patriot, who doesn't bank with Coutts,
The red hot Socialist – I don't think he'd be missed.

All those who hold that publicans it's virtuous to fleece,
And impose a heavy war tax in these piping times of peace,
And preach the code that moralists like Robin Hood held true,
That to benefit the pauper you must rob the well-to-do,
That peculiar variety of sham philanthropist,
I don't think he'd be missed, I'm sure he'd not be missed.

In his self-appointed role of (sham?) misanthropist, Gilbert gave us a blue-print for what has become, over time, a fascinating social barometer. As a vehicle for mocking the mighty, pricking the pompous, and even poking fun at oneself, the Little List has taken on a cultural life and relevance of its own.

As we have attempted to show in the following pages, the witty scalpel of the Little List has come to be wielded not only in its theatrical setting, but in many varying locations for all sorts of different reasons. But be it at a party conference, a memorial service, or in a magazine, at heart it is always respectful and amusing, nudge-nudge and never nasty.

GILBERT'S LIST FOR CHILDREN

Lest further proof were needed that Gilbert thought one set of words to be very much as good as another, in 1909 he produced an entirely new Little List for a children's version of *The Mikado*.

In this we discover that the Mikado had issued a decree that any persons who were guilty of the vulgar and detestable offence of scribbling their obscure names upon Public Monuments should forthwith be beheaded; the cheap tailor of Titipu had fallen foul of this law by writing 'Try Ko-Ko's fifteen shilling suits' on a highly venerated statue of Buddha, Titipu's favourite deity. Flirting was not mentioned…

As someday it may happen that a victim must be found,
I've made a little list – I've made a little list –
Of inconvenient people who might well be underground,
For they never would be missed – they never would be missed.
The donkey who of nine-times-six and eight-times-seven prates,
And stumps you with enquiries on geography and dates,
And asks for your ideas on spelling 'parallelogram',
All narrow-minded people who are stingy with their jam,
And the torture-dealing dentist, with the forceps in his fist –
They'd none of them be missed – they'd none of them be missed.

There's the nursemaid who each evening in curlpapers does
your hair,
With an aggravating twist – she never would be missed.

And tells you that you mustn't cough or sneeze or yawn or stare,
She never would be missed, I'm sure she'd not be missed.
All those who hold that children shouldn't have too much to eat,
And think cold suet pudding a delicious birthday treat,
Who say that little girls to bed at seven should be sent,
And consider pocket-money isn't given to be spent,
And doctors who on giving you unpleasant draughts insist –
They never would be missed – they'd none of them be missed.

Then the teacher who for hours keeps you practising your scales
With an ever-aching wrist – she never would be missed.
And children, too, who out of school are fond of telling tales,
They never would be missed – I'm sure they'd not be missed.
All people who maintain (in solemn earnest – not in joke)
That quantities of sugar-plums are bad for little folk,
And those who hold the principle, unalterably fixed,
That instruction with amusement should most carefully be mixed,
And these (and many others) I have placed upon the list,
For they never would be missed – never, never would be missed.

How little changes in a hundred years!

Above and opposite: Gilbert's own illustrations for the Little List in Songs of a Savoyard

SULLIVAN'S SCORE

We should not forget the composer!

Arthur Seymour Sullivan was born in Lambeth; his father was a military band-master from Ireland, and his mother was of Italian descent. He was a chorister at the Chapel Royal and from there won a scholarship to the Royal Academy of Music, going on to further studies in Leipzig. On his return to England in his early twenties, he began building a reputation as one of this country's most promising young composers. His first collaboration with Gilbert was *Thespis* in 1871; it was rather hastily put together and enjoyed only a little success. It took another four years before the two were brought together again, this time by Richard D'Oyly Carte; the success of *Trial by Jury* launched the two on their legendary partnership, with *The Mikado* following some ten years later.

This book is principally about text, but let there be no doubt that the composer's contribution to the success of these operas is paramount; he clearly understood Gilbert's writing and never sought to out-shine it, but merely complement it in a most positive fashion. He devised a way of accompanying patter songs which is quite brilliant – enhancing their wit and never drowning the lyrics – thus allowing the words to speak for themselves, whilst still being set to music. The Nightmare song from *Iolanthe* is perhaps the best example of this; I first heard it read as a poem, rather late at night on Radio 4 when they chose to do a programme on nightmare poetry – an excellent accompaniment for the itinerant musician returning late from a performance far from home. The accompani-

Opposite: "Seated one day at the organ"

A young Arthur Sullivan

ment is the key here, for it intensifies in each of the three verses. The Major-General's song in *The Pirates of Penzance* is a rather different kettle of fish for the fun is in the chorus response, as well as the magnificence of the language and the absurdity of the character. Sullivan manages to understand the importance of the text for each character, and finds a musical way to illustrate it. The List Song is no ordinary patter song – it is not marked 'allegro' but 'allegretto grazioso' – a far more leisurely tempo. Normally the patter song is about 'self' – 'when I was a lad'; 'when I, good friends, was called to the bar'; 'my name is John Wellington Wells'; 'I am the very model of a modern Major-General' and so on – the List Song is about other people, as we know!

To many, Sullivan's music is second-rate, but this is not an opinion I share, and I have tried to suggest his modest genius in the above paragraph. However, let me leave it to the early twentieth-century English critic Horace Thorogood to give his appreciation; let us catch up with him as he describes the impressions made on him when he first heard *The Mikado*; he was, he confesses, a musically uncultivated boy.

'There I became immediately infatuated with Sullivan and for the next few years I haunted the theatre so long as the operas remained there. My head was full of Sullivan melodies. They gave me complete content. But as these visits went on, I became aware of a new and distressing doubt arising in my mind about Sullivan. For I was now perforce hearing Wagner, Tchaikovsky, Mozart and Beethoven practically for the first time. For long I fought loyally against the conviction that these men were giants beside Sullivan, but the time came when I could deny it no longer. In the fierce glow of the great masters, my idol shivered and cracked, and finally crashed. That phase, of course, passed long since. Gradually I restored Sullivan to his true place in the galaxy of composers – no longer among the gods, yet definitely with the great. Above all, I came to realise with gratitude that it was he who prepared my mind to receive the master musicians. And this, I suggest, was one of Sullivan's greatest gifts to his countrymen. He did more than any other man to accustom the ear of ordinary Englishmen to music of pure quality – to enable them to recognise and rejoice in the finest music when they heard it. He brought the English out of the dunce's class of music.'

Sir Arthur bequeathed the original autograph full score of *The Mikado* to the Royal Academy; and reproduced with their permission in the next few pages is the List Song as it appears there. The text of only one verse appears – curiously, the version noted above that was used in the full score published in Leipzig in 1898. Another interesting point is that on page 6 we see the only evidence of the original first night list with Ko-Ko singing his own chorus which finished,

If accomplished by the nation at a reasonable charge.

This is crossed out but the final playout is left in.

The original key was D major, but the preceding number (Behold the Lord High Executioner) was in E flat, so when the position of the song was changed in the opera, so was the key.

All^mo grazioso.

No 5 a — Song. Koko.

Act I — in E♭

"A distinct gain to Society" "at large"

a distinct gain to society at large

Flauto — col Viol. I^mo

Piccolo — col Viol. I^mo

Oboe

Clar. A

Fag

Corni in E♭

Viol. I

Viol. II — pizz

Viola — pizz

Koko

2^d Voice

3^d Voice

4^h Voice

Cello — pizz

Basso — pizz

staccato
arco
p
As it seems to be es-sen-tial that a vic-tim should be found, I've got a lit-tle list – I've got a lit-tle list Of so-ci-al of-fenders who might

well be under ground – And who | never would be missed – who | never would be missed! There's the | Income tax Commis-sion-ers with | all their prying clerks. (And) | vulgar lit-tle street boys who are

'll be underground, and who | never would be missed – who | never would be missed! There's the | income tax Commissioners | all their | And | little streetboys who are

rude in their remarks; All
persons with free sen-ti-ments - a
ve-ry whole-some rule - And
next door neighbours ev-ery-where, and
boys at home from school; All
men who bite their nails, all persons
9
10
11
12
13
14
143 142

A
Col Viol. I
Col Viol I
a 2
A
Chorus of men.
1. He's got 'em on the list - He's got 'em on the list. They'll none of them be missed - They'll none of them be missed!
2.
3. You may put 'em on the list - may put 'em on the list. They'll none of them be missed - They'll none of them be missed!

Fine
na-tion If ac-
the na-tion
rea - son - a - ble
charge.
Fine.
unis

"And apologetic statesmen of a compromising kind,
Such as—What d'ye call him—Thing'em-bob, and likewise—never-mind,
And 'St—'st—'st—and What's-his-name, and also You-know-who—
The task of filling up the blanks I'd rather leave to YOU.
But it really doesn't matter whom you put upon the list,
For they'd none of 'em be missed—they'd none of 'em be missed!"

—From "The Mikado"

CONSERVATIVES

I do not intend any political statement in beginning with the Tories; simply – and through no fault of their own – they happened to be in government when this particular Ko-Ko assumed the social responsibility of compiling the Little List.

As one might expect, there was much material to work with up until the general election of May 1997. After that, their tally of entries inevitably tails off somewhat, counter-balanced by New Labour's claim to the limelight. That said, Ko-Ko was as delighted as everyone else (Tory MPs aside) to discover that their banishment to the political wilderness did little to diminish the now-infamous 'sleaze factor', and that the tattered remnants of the party continued to grab the headlines – albeit for all the wrong reasons. But we are getting ahead of ourselves...

In the beginning was the word, and the word was 'privatisation'.

> And those members of the Tory group who want to privatise
> They've sold us gas, they'll sell us air, with all the same old lies.
>
> Or those privatising Tories who'd be better off in jail
> With their latest contribution of destroying British Rail.

Of course, in case flogging the nation's assets didn't make ends meet, there was, unforgettably, a certain *per capita*...

> And finally that Poll Tax, it should be by us dismissed.
> Like that Arts Philistinist – I know she'll not be missed.

Opposite: All change? Harold Macmillan elevated to the premiership, by Vicky

The personalities of the government's front bench, mercifully, were significantly more entertaining than their policies.

> Politicians are just amateurs who like to think they can.
> And some mere opportunists, like Environment's Tarzan.
> They like to walk a tightrope with a minimum of ease
> (Remember Major's father was proficient on trapeze).

Pleasingly, Norman Lamont – John Major's successor at No. 11 – had got himself into a spot of bother involving an incautiously-chosen tenant:

> And those who rent the houses of distinguished Chancellists:
> It turns out that they are no more than strict sex therapists.

The honourable member for Winchester had similar problems (well before the Lib Dems tried to muscle in on this particular patch of turf):

> And that bent MP for Winchester who's been not too direct,
> At least his party members have the chance to deselect.

In the fullness of time, of course, Lamont was himself deselected as Chancellor, after interest rates hit the 10% mark on Black Wednesday:

> The sacking of poor Norman is a loss they can't agree on,
> But serve him right for claiming that 'Je ne regrette rien'.

Further afield, matters European were still in their infancy:

> And those who think the *écu* will replace the dear old pound,
> And supporters of the ERM (how strange these names
> do sound!).
>
> And that singular anomaly, the Channel Tunnelist,
> or the Tory Federalist
> or the friendly monetarist
> They never would be missed: *jamais* would they be missed.

The beleaguered Conservatives emerged bloodied and bowed from the 1991 election, but still nominally in power. By a miracle of good fortune, Ko-Ko was on hand the next night to deliver some incisive political commentary:

> But last night's Tory losses were not bad, they do insist;
> They're all self-delusionists and I'm sure they'll not be missed.

Determined to show that the Tories were in tune with the zeitgeist, in the early nineties a certain Minister delivered his own List to the party conference, earning him a retaliatory swing of Ko-Ko's verbal axe:

> And Lilley-livered ministers who sing from *The Mikado*,
> They'll soon be turning up in Spain to act in Eldorado.

Now, as my solicitor, how do you advise me to deal with this difficulty?

Winston, Gilbert and Sullivan

"*WE'VE got 'em on the list, there's none of them will be missed.*"—By Gittins.

Churchill in 1944

A certain level of astute topicality can work wonders in winning over an audience – the day's headlines from the *Evening Standard* being a particularly handy source of 'inspiration'. One budget gave me this opportunity:

> The budget slammed no VAT on things we like to eat
> (That tax is just for luxuries – hot water, light and heat).
>
> And that singular anomaly, the feel-good factorist,
> Kenneth Clark is on my list, he never would be missed.

Years of research reveal that audiences like nothing more than an excuse to laugh grimly at their own sufferings!

By the mid-nineties the Tories were beginning to offer us some really good characters. Alas (for both me and him) the minister for whom I had the most respect also provided the best fun;

> And football club supporters who make love with kiss-and-tellers
> Wearing all the gear for kinky fun that once was David Mellor's.

He was by far the best Arts Minister we have had in recent times, and it was a tragedy that he should have to depart from politics in such a way. Nonetheless, he has continued to support the arts in many ways, and I reprint these lines as a tribute and in admiration.

The flamboyant member for Kensington & Chelsea was having a fun time too – and keeping it in the family:

And that judge's wife and daughter who liked fun to an excess,
The naughty covenists – that's Alan Clark's new list.

As it turned out, equally strange things were going on at the top, (this was a long time before we heard of blue underpants and Mrs. Currie), but there was a smokescreen:

That '*liaison dangereuse*' with a kitchen caterer
Brings a whole new different meaning to the term a '*force majeure*'.

Skulduggery of different (if more palatable) sorts was also going on:

If Aitken's resignation claims he wants to spend more time
With his solicitists, he's welcome on my list.
And of course there's Jeffrey Archer, the insider dealerist,
And his wife on that Lloyd's list – they never would be missed.

In a subsequent trial concerning Lord Archer's acquaintance with a young lady of negotiable repute, the presiding judge evidently felt that Lady Archer had been shamefully ill-treated, and demanded of the peer how he could even consider straying emotionally from such a radiant beauty:

The outcasts now in Florida are those poor Cuban vagrants.
But here we have Lord Archer, and his wife with all that 'fragrance'.

Charles Ricketts' design for Ko-Ko, 1926

Henry Lytton in his new costume

While the judiciary worked over-time to keep matters in perspective, the torrent of revelation and scandal surrounding the party soon reached the generic stage where the naming of specific parliamentarians became unnecessary.

> But sleaze is all about us still, please do not be misled.
> For sleep there's single, double, and now Tory size of bed.

Ironically, this was all going on at as a time when the government was making much of morality:

> And those who think that censorship is getting overmuch:
> Why can't we buy decoders and turn on to Red Hot Dutch?

A string of cabinet re-shuffles – designed to reinforce the creaking bulwarks – caused as many problems as they were supposed to solve:

> The Welsh Secretary's been sent to reign in central Abyssinia –
> Just as bright as giving Heritage to Bottomley Virginia.

But with the 1997 election approaching things really began to go wrong:

> Election time is here again, we're seeing more of Norma
> Quite frankly I'd prefer a poppadom and chicken korma.

> And that latest sleazy victim – yes, the cash-for-questionsist:
> Little Willets on my list, he never would be missed.

The MP who found himself face down in Bournemouth in
the gutter:
These party conference Guinnesses did cause his brain to flutter.

There's that Kensington and Chelsea Tory man who has
been beat,
Not only is he Nicholas, he's also lost his seat.

These last pairs refer to a colourful former Northern Ireland Minister, Alan Clark's predecessor in K&C (once tipped by *Time* magazine as a future world leader!). As is so often the way, the upsets in his career are more likely to be remembered than the highpoints.

But lest it appear that West London is being singled out for unfair treatment, we should not forget

All those who want to leave their dear old spouses in a hurry,
With the possible exception of long-suffering Mr. Currie.

And those who want to keep their guns, however bad their aim is,
And members of the Cabinet who like caning 'in extremis'.

In the midst of all this embarrassment the Conservatives managed to elect a new party leader:

That baseball-hatted wunderkind, the balding Toryist,
'Don't be vague' is on my list – his hairline won't be missed.

Ko-Ko: (Mr Henry Lytton):
'Now what do you really think of these new costumes?'
Pooh-Bah (Mr Leo Sheffield):
'Come over here, where the Lord High Costumier can't hear us'

And occasionally a Tory MP even managed to score a point or two against Labour's golden boys in the House. One particular battleaxe was always a joy if not to watch then at least to listen to:

> That shadow lady spokesperson who makes us all guffaw:
> Yes, Widdecombe's the name, and for her breakfast she eats
> Straw.

But while the chattering classes should have been concerning themselves with opposition policy-making, the media seemed unwilling (tragic!) to let the Tories off the hook.

> There's that ex-Paymaster General whose memoirs are beyond hope.
> And all the shadow cabinet who've admitted smoking dope

… continued to occupy an undue number of column inches. And the catalogue of schoolboy naughtiness didn't stop there.

> When washing pots and pans it's good to use a brand new Brillo
> But more's required to clean the reputation of…Tit Willow.

Rory Bremner – all credit to him – had beaten me to the punch-line with a wonderful re-write of 'Tit Willow', substituting 'Portillo' for the eponymous hero.

Of course, other former MPs notoriously could not find enough publicity:

And that sleazy naked pair of whom we'll now have had enough
Neil and Christine won't be missed – I know they won't be missed.

While the party cringed at the shameless (but admittedly remunerative) antics of the Hamiltons, yet another Tory leader was found somewhere, and one who had to deal with even bigger skeletons in the party closet:

And that Baroness who's going at last to rest her deep bass voice
Iain Duncan Smith has said with much relief, 'Rejoice, rejoice.'

That was 2002 … Though Ko-Ko would be happy, in other circumstances, to take credit for having effected a major change in global affairs, in most instances he can but work with the material he is given: so spent were the Tories as a political force, the Lists make no further mention of them until 2006.

MRS. THATCHER'S LIST

This was transcribed from a TV programme by someone with lightning reflexes – alas I cannot credit the writer, but I applaud him and thank him belatedly for a wonderful contribution – but why should I assume that it's a 'he'?

As some day it may happen that you think I'll compromise,
I've got a little list – I've got a little list,

"AS SOME DAY IT MAY HAPPEN THAT A VICTIM MUST BE FOUND,
I'VE GOT A LITTLE LIST – I'VE GOT A LITTLE LIST..." (THE MIKADO)

Of a thousand institutions that I've still to privatise –
They never would be missed – they never would be missed.
I'm privatising sewage though it's going to lose me votes,
Because I'm very keen on selling anything that floats.
And just to show how green I am, I'm privatising air,
And then I shall proceed to privatise the ozone layer.
And destroy those lefty Bishops who are all a little hard –
I'm privatising God! I'm privatising God!

There's a certain Royal person, who has lost her former scene,
I've got her on our list – I've got her on our list.
For after all, does Britain really need a second Queen?
She never would be missed – she never would be missed.
I'll privatise the Upper-Crust, I'll privatise the Dregs,
I'll privatise your underwear, I'll privatise your legs,
I'll privatise your fingernails, I'll privatise your hair;
I'll sell Edwina Currie off at seven pence a share!
And as I meet my Maker – I'll announce with my last breath,
I'm privatising Death – I'm privatising Death!

Rejoice! Rejoice!

Opposite: Mrs. Thatcher in full flight, by Nicholas Garland

PETER LILLEY'S ATTEMPT

Such is the resonance of the Little List format as a tool for enumerating one's complaints and despatching one's enemies that many non-performers (in distinctly non-theatrical circumstances) revert to it almost automatically.

At the Conservative Party Conference in 1992, Peter Lilley gave a keynote speech on social security. Here is how he clarified Tory policy:

> As some day it may happen that a victim must be found
> I've got a little list – I've got a little list
> Of benefit offenders who I'll soon be rooting out
> And who never would be missed, they never would be missed –
> There are those who make up bogus claims in half a dozen
>   names
> And councillors who draw the dole to run Left wing campaigns,
> Young ladies who get pregnant just to jump the housing list,
> And dads who won't support the kids of ladies they have…
>   kissed.
> And I haven't even mentioned all those sponging socialists
> I've got them on my list and they'd none of them be missed.

When Paddy Ashdown stepped down from being the leader of the Liberal Democratic Party, he also found a list… and included were, of course,

Peter Lilley… and Portillo's not been missed.
Michael Howard's on my list – lots of Tories on my list.
Red Ken's on my list – but then he's on Tony's list.

Admittedly, Ashdown wanted to cut the number of MPs at Westminster by about 75%, so almost anyone memorable would have been on his list. Still, while he lacked something of the style and panache of Lilley, the points were made. Curious to note the survivor amongst them, though…

David Blunkett considered Peter Lilley's List one of his favourite conference moments ever

'I've got a little list, I've got a little list.'—*The Mikado.*

LABOUR

In my early years of List writing, the Labour party was hardly worthy of mention, and indeed there was such wrangling within the party that very little of real interest seemed to occur. (It is possible, of course, that things did occur, but, being in opposition for the duration, Labour got away with brushing them under the carpet.)

However one of the Members erred, and his preferences were aired, along with some dirty linen:

> There's the Labour MP's mistress who coined a term bizarre,
> The' knicker-nickerist' – I'm sure he'll not be missed.

In all the party wrangling, old-fashioned hardliners were being outed too:

> And both those Labour militants, T. Fields and Dave Nellist
> Oh no! That's Kinnock's list – I'm sure they'd not be missed.

Political dinosaurs were rapidly being replaced by a new breed coming into public life:

> Actors who enter politics in search of cut and thrust
> Like that Hampstead Socialist – yes, Glenda's on my list.

And then, in 1997, the inevitable happened and the world changed, largely thanks to this man:

> There's that man without portfolio the Labour Party fears,
> The crab spin-doctorist – yes, Mandy's on my list.

Opposite: Ian Mikardo (sic), left-winger and chairman of the Labour Party, 1970-71

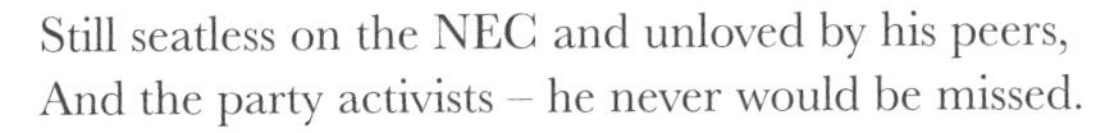

Still seatless on the NEC and unloved by his peers,
And the party activists – he never would be missed.

Everything, we were told, was going to be transparent – 'whiter than white', in fact (which is not quite the same, admittedly). What a horrifying prospect, though: was Ko-Ko in danger of running out of victims? The answer, it turned out rather quickly, was no.

Now the banning of tobacco ads is easier said than done,
Especially if your party's getting funds from Ecclestone.

And our Foreign Secretary whose good looks belie his years,
He's well behind the White House now in most of his affairs.

And there was the usual quota of gaffes from MPs who couldn't quite see how their pronouncements would look in newsprint:

There's those shops promoting loyalty cards that clog up all our purses,
And that black MP who doesn't like blond, blue-eyed, Finnish nurses.

Much was promised, but little was offered:

Star parties held at No. 10 to bolster interest
In that Tuscan Socialist – my pension's on his list.

This refers, of course, to the Great Pension Raid of 1997 that was the work of the then Chancellor (for a fuller account of whose disastrous activities see Jeff Randall's *The Clunking Fist* on p. 71).

From the beginning, Tony Blair set himself up as a target, and therefore it is only right that one should take pot-shots:

> There's that scandalous new pay-rise given to each M of P –
> It's simple to forgo it if your wife's a top QC.
>
> And that singular anomaly, the hereditary peer;
> Oh no that's Tony's list – he never would be missed.
>
> Now what of our own leader with his European kink?
> Goodbye, my dear Prime Minister, you are the weakest link.

International status beckoned…

> Let's not forget our President (the self-styled…) Tony Blair
> We've still bad schools, few trains; but he'd not know – he's never here.
> His NHS is sending poorly patients into France
> Yes, Eurostar resembles now a high-speed ambulance.

And then, of course

> … that dodgy dossier of which we're all now well aware,
> And 'sexed-up' they insist – BBC is on a list.

THE LORD HIGH EXECUTIONER ANNOUNCES THAT HE HAS "GOT A LITTLE LIST."
THE CHANCELLOR OF THE EXCHEQUER.

Above: Sir Stafford Cripps
Opposite: Harold Wilson, Prime Minister and sometime Chairman of the D'Oyly Carte Trustees

> Those weapons of mass destruction, were they really ever there?
> And George Dubya Bush's poodle what is known as Tony Blair.

Luckily for the Prime Minister, he was surrounded by a supportive family, not least

> … that lad from Number Ten who likes a drink but ends up pi….

The colourful characters will out in the span of any government, and Blair was soon surrounded by a regular posse, his own Deputy Prime Minister leading in a strong field. John Prescott initiated bus lanes on the M4, but apparently thought he himself was immune (a belief shared, tragically, by many others):

> There are those who drive in bus-lanes on our crowded
> motorways,
> (New Labour's transport policy is nothing what it says).
> And the MP known as Two Jags – was it Two Shags? – I don't
> mind,
> The croquet-mallet-ist – he's been known to use his fist.

Occasionally someone took the trouble to fight back (eggs on one occasion, a bucket of water on another), not least those who thought the New Labour party was selling out its leftist heritage:

> Like Chumbawumba's leather-mini-skirted anarchist:
> Mr Prescott wasn't missed – I don't think he was missed.

Speaking of Transport, though…

> It's Autumn time once more, and yes, the leaves are on the line,
> But so are Stephen Byers and Joe Moore, which is just fine.

... they of the 'burying bad news' on a certain day, you will recall.

> And unfortunate misunderstandings plaguing poor old Byers
> Shouldn't he be now the one to go or say that he retires?

I think he did; but others of Tony's cronies hung on:

> … the idiot who's attempting to wipe out the Lord Chancellor's post,
> (That wallpaper is good for maybe sixty years at most.)
> There's that cheeky little chappie whose pronouncements make us
>   boil;
> And ministers who're ridding us of everything that's royal –
> The people's this, the people's that; what is their real intent?
> So I'll add to my own little list 'Her Majesty's Government'.

Perhaps Ko-Ko got carried away there, but this sums up his feelings most (after all, he's just missed having his head chopped off, and he is an ex-tailor):

> There's the scourge of all things sensible that mars our daily life
> The Health-and-Safety-ist – nanny state is on my list.

Ah yes, New Labour…

—THEY'LL NONE OF THEM BE MISSED."

THE CLUNKING FIST: AN OPERA FOR BROWN'S LAST BUDGET

This list by Jeff Randall, the editor-at-large of *The Daily Telegraph*, appeared in an issue of *The Spectator* in March 2007; no need to ask why he wrote it, but how had he chosen the list format? It turns out that his grammar school Director of Music forced his class to memorise *The Pirates of Penzance*, with the Major-General's song getting forever quicker. The result is that, years later, he is somewhat reserved in his opinion of the teacher, but still enthusiastic about G&S: and, as I document elsewhere, I am always delighted with a writer who can get himself onto his own list… Jeff prefaces:

> Britain doesn't do Lord High Executioners, but if it did, Gordon Brown would probably be the best in the world. The prospect of the Chancellor in this role occurred to me while listening again to Gilbert & Sullivan's masterful satire *The Mikado*. Among the joys of W. S. Gilbert's libretto is its invitation for a contemporary version of victims. Who better to identify them than the Clunking Fist?

Ko-Ko, The Lord High Executioner (Gordon Brown)

As this year it may happen that more taxes must be found
I've got a little list – I am the Clunking Fist.
So let's start with fat-cat bosses who can shed some extra pounds
And which never would be missed, I know that they exist!

Opposite: cartoon from the Leeds Mercury, 1938, with a number of familiar gripes

There's the pestilential journalists who write the *Telegraph*,
They claim I spend and squander cash – Oh please don't make me laugh.
All home owners with mortgages, including those in flats,
I'd like to tax their pets as well, their birds, their dogs and cats.
My credo's grim so watch out all you viniculturists,
You'll pay for getting pissed – don't think that you'll be missed!

Chorus (Ed Balls, Yvette Cooper, Ed Milliband)

He's got 'em on the list – for them a nasty twist:
And they'll none of 'em be missed – Brown is a mis'rablist.

Ko-Ko

There's the toiling Polish plumber, and the others of his race
And the nerd industrialist – I'll email him my list!
And the people who smoke cigarettes and puff 'em in your face,
They never would be missed – nor will the Mammonist!
Like the dealer who earns millions, on his ghastly mobile phone,
That spiv deserves the fist, because the losses aren't his own:
And the posh chap from the public school who dines in tails and tie,
And who 'doesn't go to fox hunts, but would rather like to try';
And that singular anomaly, the business columnist –
Yes JR's on my list – I'm damned if he'll be missed!

Chorus

He's got them on the list – they'll be no escapists;
No, I don't think they'll be missed – Brown is a socialist!

Ko-Ko

And that bloke from Banff and Buchan, who just now is rather rife,
The bold Scottish Nationalist – yes Salmond's on my list!
All pensioners who worked hard and then saved for later life –
Their funds have not been missed – I'm sure they'll get the gist.
As will opposition leaders of a compromising kind,
Such as – David Cameron – Sir Ming Campbell and other, tiny minds.
There's V-A-T, and stamp duty, and petrol that's taxed too –
The cost of filling up your tanks I'd rather leave to you.
No it really doesn't look good for the British motorist
For they'd none of 'em be missed – I'll show those analysts.

Chorus

You may put them on the list – from Southend to North Uist;
And they'll none of 'em be missed – Brown is the Clunking Fist!

END OF AN ERA

As some day it may happen Ko-Ko writes of Tony Blair,
I've made a little list – I've made a little list
Of some memories I have of him I'd like us all to share,
'Cos I don't think he'd be missed (more white than white, he did insist).
That mantra – education, education, education! –
Frankly failed to boost our learning or make us a brighter nation.
He increased the general tax burden and also student loans.
The NHS got loads of cash, and motorways more cones,
No stunt was unperformed by him, no photo-op was missed.
And a son was once found pissed. I don't think he'll be missed.

He was chummy, he was upbeat, he was with it, but was hollow:
That cash-for-peeragist – I'm sure he'll not be missed.
All was new and all was young (with all the policies to follow):
A dire neophilist – I *new* he'd not be missed.
Another fine achievement was of course the mighty Dome,
A project with no substance, just an awful lot of foam.
More money here, more money there, to spend was his big goal.
He delighted, too, in spinning, but it got out of control.
His deputy was hand-picked for he liked to use his fist:
That great malapropist – old two shags won't be missed.

There's those holidays in starry homes like that of Berlusconi:
Cliff Richard's on his list – Congratulationsist.

The House of Lords was cleansed unless one claimed to be a crony –
Derry Irvine's on the list: that wall-paper won't be missed.
Now those weapons of mass destruction, they were never really there:
Yes, Iraq will be his legacy – Alas, poor poodle Blair!
Then that modest farewell world tour at the tax-payers' expense –
Pope Benedict, Gaddafi, tribal chiefs? It made no sense –
But his final act of treachery he just could not resist:
He endorsed the clunking fist, that devilutionist.

LIBERALS

Although it is no surprise that the Lib Dems get rather fewer lines than the other main parties in Westminster (a cynic might say it was in keeping with their share of the vote), it is nonetheless startling to note just how little attention Ko-Ko thought they deserved throughout the late eighties and nineties.

David Steel was in the audience one night and heard:

> And finally the Democrats whose party is deceased,
> They'd none of them be missed – they'd none of them be missed.

But so it proved. Neither Lib nor Dem was mentioned for another thirteen years until their leader elicited a mention:

> There's that newly-wed MP now who is slightly worse for wear,
> The Lib Dem leaderist – that Scotch'll not be missed.

Sharp political analysts will note, of course, that this 2003 mention has precious little to do with politics (or, at least, with policy). So one was inclined to be somewhat sympathetic when, try as they might to get attention for their good work, the Lib Dems proved totally incapable of avoiding the limelight when things went badly. And in 2006, things went very badly indeed.

> The ex-leader of the Lib Dems who was hounded by the press:
> Two bottles of malt whisky is not drinking to excess.

And the other who has done something politically verboten,
(He frequented a rent-boy just to get more of his oaten).

And definitely the one who swinging both ways does insist;
Simple Simon's on my list – this is the pinkest list.

At the risk of allowing the one party to hog a disproportionate number of lines, the whole list concluded:

And that man whose shoelace tripped him whilst museum-
visiting,
A pile of broken china is now all that's left of Ming.

Which brings us back to Lib Dems (no, I really can't resist
To put them on my list) – they'd none of them be missed.

Hanki-Panki Jo:
Joseph Chamberlain as Nanki-Poo,
by Carruthers Gould

MIKADO
SH-H-H!
I CAN'T ALLOW YOU TO PLAY "THE MIKADO!"
HUSH! NOT "THE MIKADO" PLEASE
OUT OF CONSIDERATION TO THE FEELINGS OF THE JAPANESE I MUST FORBID YOU TO PLAY "THE MIKADO"
STOP, PLEASE! OUR FRIENDS THE JAPANESE WOULD FEEL HURT IF THEY HEARD YOU PLAYING "THE MIKADO"
!!!!
JAPANESE BAND PLAYING "THE MIKADO" ON BOARD A JAPANESE WARSHIP!
W. K. HASELDEN.

Ko-Ko may have humble origins, but he sees no reason why he should be restricted to carrying out his duties in a parochial manner. He has swung his axe in an international direction many times over the years, and will continue to do so (until all miscreants are cowed into good behaviour).

Contenders come from far and wide, to compete for space on the Little List. In the late eighties there was trouble in the homeland of the Mikado himself:

> There's that Japanese Prime Minister who's been a naughty Nip –
> I think those gorgeous geisha girls are right to seek a tip.

The Foreign Office made no attempt to censor these lines, though in 1907 there had been a fit of the vapours over the visit of Crown Prince Fushimi of Japan, and the Lord Chamberlain announced an indefinite ban on all performances of the opera on the grounds that it was offensive to the Japanese. MPs protested, Haselden produced the cartoon reproduced opposite, and in the event the ban only lasted six weeks. Fun was still to be had, for when the Prince was taken on endless tours of Royal Navy ships, the bands all played selections from *The Mikado*... Gilbert was knighted shortly afterwards and commented that before long 'we shall probably be at war with Japan about India, and they will offer me a high price to permit *The Mikado* to be played.'

As to whether *The Mikado* is popular in Japan, I cannot truthfully say, though I know that audiences at the Coliseum are often swelled by

INTERNATIONAL POLITICIANS

Viscount Althorp, the Lord Chamberlain, suppresses The Mikado, by W. K. Haselden, 1907

The Mikado in a Japanese production of 1948 meets Prince Nobuthito, brother of the Emperor Hirohito

Japanese tourists who presumably have come to pay homage to their emperor… they doubtless leave the theatre a little bemused. However things Japanese were extremely popular in the 1880s with the setting up of a Japanese village in Knightsbridge – fabrics and dresses were all the rage; and so Gilbert was merely cashing in on a fashion when taking his humour to the Far East, as he had already done for instance in *Patience* with aestheticism. (He did take trouble to be authentic however, employing the inhabitants of the Knightsbridge village to teach actors Japanese deportment and the expressive use of the fan; and some of the costumes were genuine Japanese antiques.)

I have only ever received one fan letter from Japan, some years back, after a recording of *The Mikado* was released there – the lady informed me that she delighted in 'Tit Willow' which she had recently heard being played in her local record store – I treasure it!

Some international visitors are not always so welcome. In 1998 the UK played host to a certain South American dictator, wanted in his own country (and a fair few others) for crimes committed. Though he'd been – and remained – big pals with Mrs Thatcher, it was Jack Straw who let Pinochet stay a while as he was 'unwell'. But when Pinochet departed, Straw was left looking either complicit, or extremely naïve, or both:

> …that fraudulent dictator who is well out of our clutches,
> He got back home to Chile and forgot to use his crutches.

And sticking with dictators (a theme, not a foreign policy):

> There's that man who tries at length his nuclear weapons
> to conceal;
> It's outrageous that his people can't afford a proper meal.

Of course, it is well known that one cannot libel the dead; but perhaps we ought to acknowledge that, in the end, it transpired that Mr Hussein did not, in fact, have any nuclear weapons. Still, anyone could have made that mistake, eh?

Mainland Europe is a constant source of ready-made fun, be it the French…

> And those Frenchmen who are popular like ooh aah Cantona,
> One really can't imagine chanting Jacques Chirac la la;
> But we made him eat the beef, at least the Queen she did insist,
> BSE is on my list, I'm sure that won't be missed.

… or the Italians. Signor Berlusconi is mentioned elsewhere, but more specifically in 2004, alongside:

> Those accountants down at Parmalat whose figures were quite
> phoney –
> Just like the plastic surgery enjoyed by Berlusconi.

When Boris Yeltsin was in charge of Russia, Kremlin life was quite unpredictable. He was once supposed to have a stop-over in Ireland on the way back from the USA for talks with Irish politicians; strangely, though, he never made it out of the plane.

> And Yeltsin had so much to drink, the Blarney was not kissed –
> Quite obviously pi….

The whole European business has always been something of a comedic turkey-shoot, from

> Those Common Market ministers in Maastricht for a chat:
> We could get a better fudge at home… and tastier at that.

… to

> Those European heads of state who met down in Madrid.
> Their communiqués are pure whitewash: of them we should
> get rid.

But it is generally from the USA that we get the most amusement. In 2000 (as in every other Olympic year), we were all totally fed up with the presidential race to The White House:

> American elections now are really such a bore –
> Who gives a dimpled chad who wins, but please not Bush or Gore.

One of them did win, alas, becoming President despite the fact that he had trouble getting food into his mouth without mishap:

And that Texan who quite simply on a pretzel tried to choke –
Chew'n'swallow, he insists – that shrub'll not be missed.

Bush's Vice-President joined an inglorious catalogue of blundering Number Twos one wet afternoon:

When shooting quail it's good to pick a day that's not too rainy,
And be careful who you go with – just make sure it's not
Dick Cheney.

Still, for entertainment value few could compete with Bill Clinton, who livened up our breakfast tables enormously towards the end of his time in office (offering us proof, if proof were needed, that Americans don't like a brain in their Presidents – and human weaknesses they just can't stand). To Clinton's most infamous cock-up, Ko-Ko responded, in admiration:

And I really have to mention dear Miss Monica Lewinsky –
Whose blue dress was so handy when she took it on her chinsky.

But when it comes to international affairs, it doesn't get much more serious than

Those caber-tossing, bag-pipe-blowing Celts from way up North:
The Scottish Nationalists – they never would be missed.
They wheel out ex-pat actors to proclaim the Firth of Forth:
007sh on my lisht – Dr No, he'd not be mished.

An advertisement for the 1938 film - never used!

MAO'S LITTLE LIST

The first two man show ever to be billed at the Coliseum did not take place until 1969, when the honour fell to the argumentative duo of Sir William Goldberg and Sir Arthur Solomon, fresh from their tour of South Africa. Though heavily outnumbered by the stage hands – those were the days – they brought the house down in a benefit for the Sadler's Wells Benevolent Fund, performing a series of numbers from their many operas – *M. R. S. Pinafore: or, The Story of Sarah Schmuttercup and her Wholesale business with the sailors in Portsmouth*; *The Tailors of Poznance: or, The Apprentice Lover should never press his suit in the firm's time;* and *The Chandeliers*, a touching story of two gay interior decorators painting a Duke's palace in Majorca.

Undoubtedly the prime offering, from our point of view, on that historic Coliseum night, was *The (you should excuse me) Pigtails of the Three Little Maids from Shule.* This was set in Red China, where Shmoko, the Jewish Ambassador to the Court of Chairman Mao Tse Shtoom, has to deal with the Chairman's elderly, ugly daughter, Chazershe r('pig-face'), who is rather fond of Hanky Panky, a wandering Milkman.

In this version it is the Mikado Mao who gets to sing the Little List:

Every day I go out searching through the streets and through
the ports
I've got a little list!
He's got a little list!

And I write down names of people who have never read my
thoughts
Although they do insist they're a faithful communist.
There's the two faced politicians who think Joe Stalin's right
But they won't back the Egyptians every time they want to fight
All people who are democrats as though there's nothing finer
And greet me without due respect by saying "Wotcher, China!"
I've got a place for all of these, on that I do insist
I've got them on my list, I've got them on my list.
He's got them on his list, he's got them on his list
And they'll none of 'em be missed, they'll none of 'em be missed.

Then there's L. B. J. from Washington, of whom you've doubtless
heard,
He'll soon be off my list!
(Yes, he'll soon be off his list!)
And that person that he married, yes, they called her 'Lady Bird',
I'm sure she'll not be missed – no, she never would be missed.
Then there's England's Harold Wilson, he says he's a socialist?
And his erstwhile foreign secret'ry, who's permanently....
inebriated!
And the atheist who will admit in secret to a pal
That ev'ry night he says prayers to Monsieur le Général!

Roy Cowen and Iain Kerr as Sir William Goldberg and Sir Arthur Solomon; they toured their show worldwide for ten years until Roy's untimely death in 1978

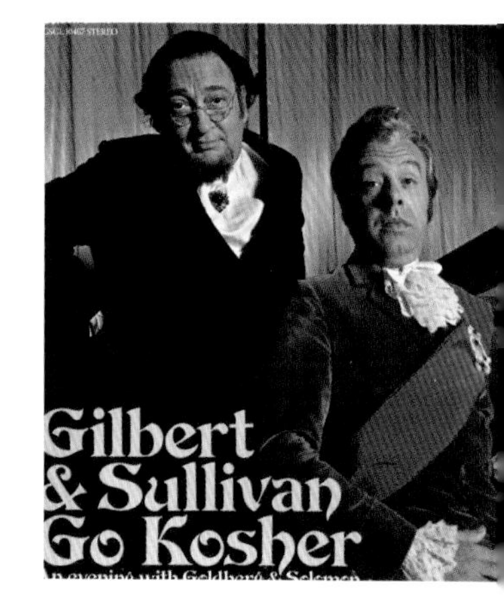

Not only are they written down – to them I'll show my fist –
I've got them on my list – yes, I've got them on my list!
Yes he's got them on his list – he's got them on his list,
And they'll none of 'em be missed – they'll none of 'em be missed.

There's that Mrs. Richard Burton, with her jewel'ry and her yachts!
Oo – I've got her on my list!
Yes, he's got her on his list!
There's the Bee Gees and the Beatles, and there's Twiggy with
her spots –
She's a-l-m-o-s-t on my list.
Well, she's j-u-s-t upon his list!
Now the western world is decadent – it's evil and defiled:
The things that they've made legal now would make poor
Oscar wild!
I'm determined to eradicate democracy and soon
My hammer and *my* sickle will be flying on the moon!
And anyone who says that they're a ca-pit-a-list
I've got them on my list – in fact you're *all* upon my list!!
(Yes, he's got 'em on his list – he's got em on his list!)
And I'll hang them by the wrist – yes!!!!
Cos they're all upon his list!

Gilbert and Sullivan as seen by Punch *when* The Mikado *opened in 1885. Gilbert sports D'Oyly Carte on his fan; Sullivan, enigmatically, a swan and a crocodile*

A NIXON LIST

From China to Nixon: this wonderful parody is by John Hollander, one of America's finest poets and literary critics. He wrote this as a favour to a friend and it appeared in the New York magazine in June 1973 together with David Levine's menacing cartoon of Richard Nixon (overleaf). Hollander, who is now Poet Laureate of Connecticut and Sterling Professor Emeritus of English at Yale University, first earned a living writing sleeve notes for classical LP's; and he has written nostalgically of seeing his first *Mikado* as a child – with Martyn Green as Ko-Ko. I am indebted to him for allowing me to reprint his work here

Of the Prominent and Distinguished who have made poor Nixon
cross
He's got a little list, he's got a little list –
Writers, businessmen and actors unadoring of the Boss
Adorn his little list, and *they* really would be missed;
And therefore to be fair we've drawn a list up of our own,
Of Enemies both far and near the Presidential Throne –
From the giddy little Liddy and the Honorable Hunt
And the unemployed ex-Cubans who performed their cheesy
stunt
To the gang of loyal lawyers who, despite (we must insist)
Their great deeds for God and Country, will never quite be
missed.

We've got them on the list –we've got them on the list,
And they'll none of 'em be missed – they'll none of 'em be missed.

The devout and brave Magruder waving copies of Thoreau's
Civil Disobedience – hssst! We've got him on our list;
And the middle men and Strachans – mighty warriors,
mighty foes –
They'll none of 'em be missed – they'll none of 'em be missed.
Then, *auf Deutsch*, the brilliant Buzhardt, sagest counsel he,
and wise,
Pulling for the *Nixonbund* and its not-yet-unfaithful guys:
The fine-toned, noble Ehrlichman, so very aptly named,
The profound and thoughtful Haldeman who *scarcely* can
be blamed
And the Ziegler feeding garbage to the craven journalist,
After all, they won't be missed – we suspect they won't be missed.

Though they get slapped on the wrist, we have put them on our list,
And they'll none of 'em be missed – they'll none of 'em be missed.

The sometime head of Justice, sometime Partner in the Law –
Such a pious moralist – we've got him on the list.

Opposite: note President Nixon's erect toe – a bit of Ko-Ko 'business' traced back to George Thorne in New York, though later claimed by Henry Lytton as his own idea

And his loud canary Martha, outrage sticking in her craw
As they give the gag a twist – well, she's fun and *might* be missed.
Colson, Mardian, Dean, Krogh; Caulfield ever watchful, lest the lax
I.R.S. fail to collect each dollar of dissenting tax,
Brave Segretti, and now spill-the-beans LaRue, oily no more–
All those great over-achievers knocking at the White House door;
Like a nasty dermal fungus, or a deeply painful cyst,
They really won't be missed, they really won't be missed.

And with luck, the brilliant jurist (what's his name? – it rhymes with 'list')
Even he would not be missed; no, they'll none of 'em be missed.

TAKE HIM OFF THE LIST,
"For he never would be missed."

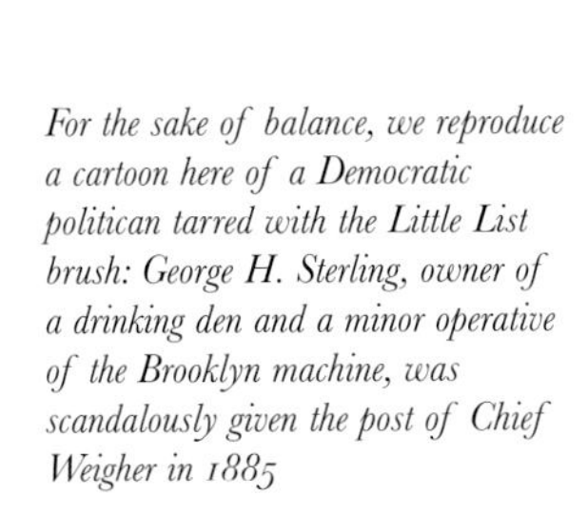
For the sake of balance, we reproduce a cartoon here of a Democratic politican tarred with the Little List brush: George H. Sterling, owner of a drinking den and a minor operative of the Brooklyn machine, was scandalously given the post of Chief Weigher in 1885

There is no question that what we know now as the American Musical really came into being as a result of that country's love for the works of Gilbert and Sullivan. Indeed it could be argued that the works are more highly treasured on the other side of the Atlantic than they are here – musical theatre there is treated more seriously as an art form; and in one of his early television shows Danny Kaye saluted their contribution thus:

> Once, long ago, before Lerner and Lowe,
> Before Porter, or Gershwin, or Rodgers,
> Most of the tunes with the 'moons' and the 'Junes'
> Were composed by two old English codgers.

Historians of the genre have been generous in their praise; John Bush Jones sees Gilbert and Sullivan as 'the primary progenitors of the twentieth century American musical.' He points out too that G&S led the way in showing that musicals can address contemporary social and political issues whilst still being entertaining.

They were also perhaps the first to establish a parity between composer and lyricist – their names are now inseparable, like Rodgers and Hammerstein. It is also interesting to note that writers are the practitioners who more readily acknowledge the influence of the Savoy operas on their own work. 'We all come from Gilbert,' admits Johnny Mercer. Alan Jay Lerner in his book *The Musical Theatre: a celebration* writes that 'Gilbert was the Adam of modern lyric writing. P. G.Wodehouse, Lorenz

Above and overleaf: In the 1950s and 60s the Bell System of America sponsored a now legendary series of musical programmes on NBC, among which was a Mikado *condensed to the obligatory TV-hour with Groucho Marx as Ko-Ko; it was adapted and directed by Martyn Green.*

the
MIKADO
on the
HOUR
29

Hart, Cole Porter, Ira Gershwin, Oscar Hammerstein and their contemporaries and descendants all owe their lyrical, genetic being to W. S. Gilbert.'

The immense popularity of G&S in the States came at a price. In the days before international copyright laws were drawn up, pirated productions of the works appeared all over the USA; an attempt to put a stop to this involved staging the first performance of *The Pirates of Penzance* at the Bijou Theatre, Paignton the night before another branch of the D'Oyly Carte Company actually premièred the show in New York.

The Mikado was a hit from the word go and became so popular that one evening in 1886 there were said to have been 170 separate performances across the USA. Richard D'Oyly Carte had five companies touring North America, four in Britain and another touring Europe.

A small and extremely rare reminder of how quickly the show entered public consciousness is a wonderful parody of the whole piece described as *The Texas Mikado* and written in 1888; it simply extols the virtues of the city of Fort Worth unashamedly – Nanki-Poo becomes Yankee-Doo, in love with By-Gum, and Pish Tush is Push-Much (a real estate dealer) – I think you get the gist… Our hero is Kokonut, who 'failed in business and was on the tramp; but he was arrested here while stealing a ride on a cattle train, and having a few dollars left, he bought an option on a Main Street lot and was soon in affluent circumstances.'

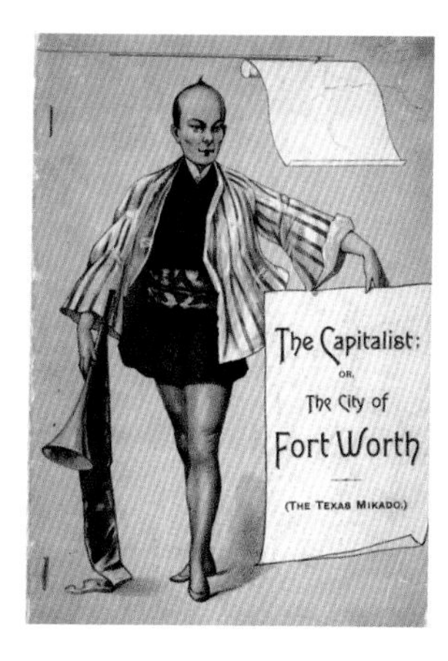

The Capitalist:
OR,
The City of
Fort Worth
(THE TEXAS MIKADO.)

"FOR HE'S GOING TO STAY IN FORT WORTH,"—YOU BET!

Kokonut

As it very often happens that I want a piece of ground,
I've got a little cash – I've got a little cash,
And the best place to invest it I quite recently have found,
And there I've got a mash – and there I've got a mash.
I have travelled o'er the country and invested everywhere,
But to this place all the others cannot in the least compare;
For it's got the climate, water, and the best location too;
Society and colleges, and churches not a few;
And here I place my surplus cash to help to swell the list,
For it never will be missed – it never will be missed.

Chorus

He'll help to swell the list – he'll help to swell the list
His cash will not be missed – it never will be missed.

Kokonut

It has thirty thousand people and in less than two years more,
(I beg that you will list – for this must not be missed),
The city's population without doubt will double o'er.
It's down upon the list – and on it I insist.
It has near a dozen railroads, which a Union depot greets;
Substantial sidewalks, sewerage, and miles of graded streets.

Opposite: Fort Worth as seen in The Texas Mikado*: all very inviting, but the cross-roads look decidedly dodgy. Due prominence is given to Joseph H. Brown's wholesale grocery warehouse; this business went bust the year after the brochure was published*

> The money for improvements of all kinds is quickly raised,
> And at the city's enterprise the State is oft amazed.
> And now I'll tell you where it is, this garden spot of earth,
> It's in Tarrant County, Texas, and its name it is Fort Worth.
>
> The garden spot of earth – the garden spot of earth,
> Is in Tarrant County, Texas, and its name it is Fort Worth.

Every page of the brochure carries encouraging footnotes about the reality of Fort Worth. On this page they read:

> The Fort Worth Board of Trade Building, when completed, will cost $100,000.
> One hundred and fifty artesian wells, ranging from 150 to 300 feet in depth, supply Fort Worth with the purest and most healthful drinking water; these wells never fail.
> One hundred tons of ice per day are made in Fort Worth from pure artesian water.
> The Fort Worth system of public schools is equal to that of any city in the United States.

KO-KO IN NEW YORK

In August 2001, I was in New York to begin rehearsals for *The Mikado* with New York City Opera: they had hired the ENO production, set, costumes, Ko-Ko and all (though I was a fairly late booking after the usual actor search), and the show was scheduled to open on 15th September.

On 3rd September, I flew back to Europe to honour an engagement I had with my friends at Diva Opera. We were to give my production of *Trial by Jury* in front of The Princess Royal, in Lausanne, as part of a charity concert on 5th September. This also happened to be my 50th birthday: no better way to spend it, I thought (if I was going to have to work at all), and I was looked after wonderfully. The following day I journeyed back to the U.S. for final stage rehearsals.

And then came 11th September.

I got up, and put on the New York news TV channel to get the weather forecast for the day; but, as could be seen from the TV Channel's permanent camera on top of the Empire State Building, the day's clear blue skies were interrupted by a plume of smoke issuing from a World Trade Centre Tower…

After only a few minutes, a friend of mine in Atlanta telephoned my wife at home in the UK, where it was already the early afternoon. He asked casually where I was at present: was I still in New York? My wife managed to get a quick call to me before 9.30 EST, and then the international lines went dead.

We were not due to rehearse that day, and the following day's calls were cancelled; but our Dress Rehearsal was due on 13th September, and went ahead as scheduled. My Little List, however, was radically changed.

Here's how the third verse would have been:

> There's that Texan who threw Kyoto out without the slightest
> thought
> The world pollutionist – I've got him on my list.
> (His daughters like their alcohol, but frequently get caught
> When trying to get pi.. – I don't think they'll be missed)
> His intellect is second to none, his oratory's delightful,
> His commanding use of language is so positively frightful;
> The dimpled chad elected him, with help, too, from his brother,
> Quite how he reached the White House, we shall prob'ly not
> discover.
> He's the lone vacation taker – the Texan executionist
> George Dubya's on my list – that shrub'll not be missed.

While it is generally perceived that you can get away with much more in song than in straight speech, it was clear that this Little List was dead in the water. All the late night TV chat shows were off air, as indeed were the live comedians: in the state of uncertainty that immediately followed 9/11 we all had to give politicians the benefit of the doubt, and I had to resort to some old and well-loved lines to get through.

Here's that same verse re-written for when we opened on 15th September 2001.

> There's our friends at Lincoln Center who love us with all
> their hearts,
> The Met is on my list, I don't think they'd be missed.
> And those who must do monologues on female body parts,
> I've got them on my list – I'd like to see their list.
> Now cleaning up Times Square is an idea that's fantastic,
> But poor old 42nd Street's just a Disney World of plastic.
> And all those TV shows where hosts are drinking mugs of tea,
> And Jerry Springer too, whose guests behave appallingly.
> And lastly that doyenne of taste, the TV chic artiste,
> It's a good thing, she insists, Martha Stewart's on my list.

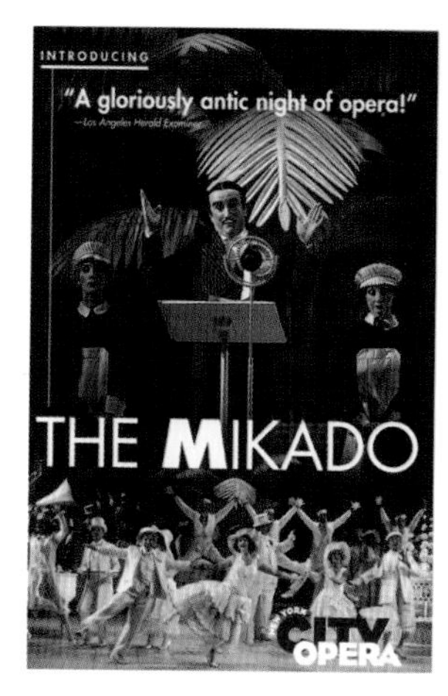

Publicity card used by City Opera, 2001

Of course the whole story of *The Mikado* is based on executions, with a Titipudlian legal code stating that if a married man was to beheaded, his wife was to be buried alive. This was felt to be a bit close to home for New Yorkers at that time, and David Ritch (Jonathan's astute assistant director who had remounted the production), came up with the alternative of Yum-Yum having to be beheaded too. This worked well enough that it was kept in when the production returned to New York in 2003.

When you make your debut with City Opera they give you a cup,

and I reprint below the text of a letter that accompanied that gift from Paul Kellogg, then the General and Artistic Director:

> Dear Richard,
>
> This debut cup commemorates the occasion and comes with the gratitude we all feel for the professionalism and understanding and gift you have brought this company in a time that has been desperately hard for us all. You have helped make this a wonderful show, and we hope that at least some of your memories of this time at City Opera will be focused on that fact.

The first night was indeed extraordinary. The whole company – singers, dressers, accountants, stage-hands, and secretaries – met on stage before curtain-up. Paul made a most moving speech and then we all, audience and performers, joined in *The Star-Spangled Banner*, during which, for the very first time in its history, the cream set of *The Mikado* was bedecked with the Stars and Stripes. After this magical moment of bonding, we set about doing the performance.

I had an English friend in New York at the time, attending a conference. On 11th September he as a doctor knew exactly what he had to do, and did it. I knew not at all what to do, but just felt the futility of my profession in such circumstances. After a week, however, I fully understood

With Sarah Walker as Katisha

KOKO.
50
BEST SIX CORD
AS THE BEST OF SPOOL COTTON YOU MAY DESIRE TO BUY
I'VE GOT A LITTLE LIST– I'VE GOT A LITTLE LIST–
AND NUMBER ONE UPON IT, COATS' SIX CORD. YOU MUST TRY
YOU'LL BE SORRY IF YOU'VE MISSED–YOU'LL BE SORRY IF YOU'VE MISSED–
IT'S STRONGER AND MUCH SMOOTHER AND MORE ELASTIC TOO
THAN ANY OTHER ONE THAT I CAN RECOMMEND TO YOU.
IF YOU'VE GOT "COATS," ALL OTHER THREADS I'VE GOT UPON MY LIST
WOULD NONE OF THEM BE MISSED–THEY'D NONE OF THEM BE MISSED

American trade card, based on George Thorne as Ko-Ko, D'Oyly Carte, New York, 1886

what was required of me: New Yorkers had to be taken away from their television sets and the gloom of the here-and-now. They had to be transported to another land, and where better than Titipu? Mayor Giuliani was in total agreement and led the way.

Returning just over two years later, I found a New York noticeably changed. But despite the omnipresent security staff and barriers, that wonderful sense of freedom was still prevalent, and so it was business as usual for Ko-Ko.

> There's that radio commentator who is such a hypocrite,
> With all those pills a-poppin' he's a stupid little… twit.
> And that wedding of the century of which much has been said,
> Is it on or off, are Jen and Ben afflected in the head?
> And then of course the Red Socks, who to name I can't resist,
> They're all upon my list, I don't think they'll be missed.
>
> There's that country which on using the pound Sterling does
> insist,
> The UK's on my list, I don't think we'll be missed.
> Let's not forget the French who being awkward can't resist,
> Jacques Chirac is on my list, French Fries will not be missed.
> Now, Arnold was a naughty boy, but should we let it rest?
> Of all his torrid groping I just cannot keep abreast.

That election on the West Coast, yes, some substance it did lack,
He frightened them by warning 'Kahleefornya, I'll be back.'
And once more that presenter and insider dealerist,
Martha Stewart's on my list, I'm sure she'll not be missed.

There's that Lincoln Centre Orchestra who wanted to take flight,
The Philharmonic's on my list, I think they might be missed.
And the chef who likes to 'kick it up a notch' before a bite,
Yes, Bam is on my list, I don't think he'll be missed.
And that New York Stock Exchange Chief who is going out to Grass-oh,
His compensation deal has made him seem a silly ass-oh.
And those weapons of mass destruction, were they really ever there?
And also Bush's lapdog who is known as Tony Blair.
And that singular anomaly the US pacifist,
Rummy Rumsfeld's on my list, I'm sure he'll not be missed.

A EUROPEAN LIST

Now, back to the United States of Europe and straight to its decision-making heart.

In 1998 I had to entertain, in an after-dinner fashion in London, a large group of European Union back-room boys and the like from Brussels – obviously part of their preparation for the evening had been to concoct their own Little List which was faxed to me shortly before the event – they evidently had axes to grind…

There's the Franco-German duo who imagine they're the boss,
We wish they would desist – we've got them on the list;
And all who speak of leadership, they make us very cross,
They'd none of 'em be missed – they'd none of 'em be missed.
And political Directors who express themselves at length,
Or imagine that the Union plays a role of global strength;
We can think of Nordic patriots who dream, of their
'dimensions',
And of southern empire-builders with their Euro-Med
extensions;
And worst of all the nation-states, who think they still exist,
They'd none of 'em be missed – we know they'd not be missed.

And the Council Legal Service gives you fifty reasons why
They drive you round the twist – we've got them on the list.

And the chap who lists the speakers, but who fails to catch your
eye,
He never will be missed – they'll none of 'em be missed.
We love our Correspondents – so much brighter than their
masters,
But they miss the vital linkage and they lead us to disasters;
Then we ask the Secretariat to save us from the flame,
And they draft a declaration for the Council to proclaim;
So we turn to the Commission who must surely head the list,
I don't think they'd be missed, I'm sure they'd not be missed.

Ko-Ko, Yum-Yum and Nanki-Poo,
by Charles E. Brock, 1928

AN EARLY GERMAN VERSION

In 1988 I auditioned for the 'new' D'Oyly Carte. The company had ceased to exist in 1982, after failing to get Arts Council funding; but a legacy from Dame Bridget D'Oyly Carte had enabled their revival under the inspired baton of Bramwell Tovey and the leadership of Dick Condon, who had made the Theatre Royal in Norwich such a success.

Auditions took place at the Savoy Theatre, and we were to prepare something from either *The Yeomen of the Guard* or *Iolanthe*, which were the two pieces going into production. Alas, I knew the patter songs from neither of these works, so cheekily went on stage with Bunthorne, as I had understudied him at English National Opera four years previously. The auditioning panel was not amused, but recalled me for three weeks hence, with the instruction that I was to have learnt 'The Nightmare Song' by then.

Well, I packed it into my suitcase and immediately left for Gelsenkirchen where I was rehearsing Peter Maxwell Davies' *Eight Songs for a Mad King* (or, as they would have it out there, *Acht Gesänge für einen verrückten König*). I began to learn the Lord Chancellor in one of their music practice rooms, and all too soon somebody poked his head round the door. 'Mein Gott, Richard, was ist das?' I explained briefly that it was from a work by Gilbert & Sullivan, was extremely English and concerned itself with the House of Lords, knowing that I would find little recognition. 'Gilbert und Sullivan – ich habe von sie nie gehört!'

Opposite: Julius Lieban, a famous German Ko-Ko

That did not come as a great shock: in a country which boasts so much culture and so many opera houses, I know that the Savoy operas are only rarely performed (though *Die Piraten von Penzance* was seen recently in Berlin, and I am in contact with a charming couple who are responsible for performances in Switzerland).

I was intrigued therefore to come across the libretto – in wonderful old German – of *Der Mikado oder Ein Tag in Titipu*, described as a Burlesk-Operette in zwei Akten. It is translated by one Dr C. Carlotta, and was published in 1886 in Berlin, just one year after the British première. Here are the first lines of the German 'Little List'.

Im Fall, daß 'mal ein Opfer nöthig für mein Richterſchwert
:,: So erſann ich eine Liſt :,:
Machte ein Verzeichniß derer, die das Leben gar nicht werth,
:,: Und die niemals man vermißt :,:

The translation of these lines follows much of Gilbert's original, though 'society offenders' he finds hard to work, and so in the third line he 'makes a list of all those who are not worthy to be alive.'

So zum Beiſpiel Leute, die uns ſtets von einem wicht'gen Gang
Aufhalten durch Erzählungen, fünf Viertelſtunden lang;

He now departs from the original and lists 'for example people who natter on forever with self-important stories' and

Julius Lieban
von der Berliner Hofoper als
einer der drolligſten Kokos

Der Freund, der stets den „neu'sten" Witz vergnüglich colportirt,
War er zu Zeiten Meidingers bereits auch antiquirt,

'That friend who always recites the 'latest' joke – one which however was old hat even in Meidinger's day.' Meidinger was a professor of physics who did his most important work some years before this: intellectual stuff, German humour! The first verse finishes with 'the partner in the card game whist who gives away trump cards':

Der Partner, der bei unserm Stich Atout zugiebt im Whist —
:,: Sie würden nie vermißt! :,:

It is in the second verse, though, that we begin to see the true colours of Dr Carlotta.

Auch für alle Dilettanten maltraitirend ein Clavier
:,: Gebraucht ich meine List :,:
Die den Wein mit Wasser taufen und verplantschen unser Bier
:,: Die würden nie vermißt! :,:

He lists dilettantes who abuse the piano and (now the crucial bit…) those who dilute wine or water down the beer – ah yes, he got his priorities right! His last verse follows Gilbert by and large, in particular the last six lines which are readily understood:

> Und die Herrn im Parlamente, welche stets so wüthend schrein,
> So wie — wie nennt er sich — Herr Dingsda, der Nam' fällt mir nicht
> Und Pst! Pst! Pst! und Herr von X und — ach! was weiß denn
> Da muß ich bitten, füllen Sie aus den Gedankenstrich;
> Aber brauchen Sie, bei wem Sie wollen, dreist nur meine List:
> Nicht Einer wird vermißt, 's wird Keiner je vermißt!

KO-KO AT LA FENICE

Unlikely as it may be, but in 2002 the ENO *Mikado* was shipped over to Venice for five performances. This was a first for the Fenice company, though not for Italy: there had been a production – in Italian – in Palermo, in 1991 (see p. 115). But surtitles, of course, can take us anywhere now (even if one might have thought that *The Gondoliers* would have been more apt).

The Fenice opera house itself was still being rebuilt, so performances were taking place in a large marquee that had been installed on the island of Tronchetto. If you arrive in Venice by coach, this is where you get deposited before continuing your journey by vaporetto. It made for an interesting juxtaposition. The auditorium was very large and the entire structure could easily accommodate the set – indeed it looked most impressive, standing as it did on a stage that was raised over what had been a car park (no pit for the orchestra, just tarmac). The wonderful thing about the whole positioning, however, was that, when they were not playing, the orchestral members could see both the stage and the surtitles, and were able to join in the fun of the production. For their part, the Italian chorus were in seventh heaven: when before had they been able to learn a Charleston for use in a show? Or to wear a gymslip, for that matter? And the entire stage was bathed in bright light: no mysterious corners for murder and the like, no spears to carry, just jolly hockey sticks and elegant black and white costumes.

When it came to the Little List, I wanted to do a verse in Italian, naturally. By a piece of good fortune I had met, some months earlier, a true European by the name of Davide Traxler, in Switzerland. He was fluent in several languages, including Italian, so I asked him to write me a verse, which he was delighted to do. He warned me though that I must be very even-handed about politicians, and he concocted several sets of lines with this in mind. I eventually agreed on what follows, and rehearsed this on several occasions in run-throughs back in Venice.

We reached the Dress Rehearsal and, during the overture, as I was putting on my make-up, David Ritch came into my dressing room looking rather pale. He had just been summoned to the highest office at La Fenice and told that he must inform me not to use my verse for the first two performances. The authority claimed that, as this was the first time that the opera had been seen in Venice, only the original Gilbert would do. David likes telling the story of what I said next… but the reality was that never in my life had I sung the original last verse, let alone memorised it – and what was more, I was not sure I could lay my hands on the preferred text in the next ten minutes.

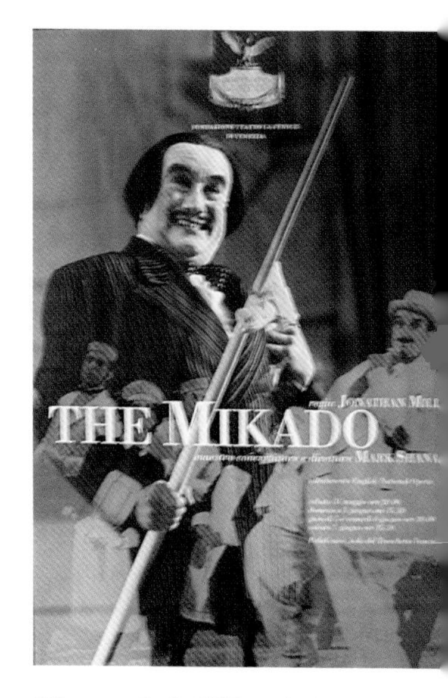

The poster for the ENO production in Venice

The truth was more sinister though, and very Italian. Signor Berlusconi, the then Prime Minister and a man of dubious business dealings, had a hand in everything from newspapers to television companies to arts funding. The Intendant was (perhaps correctly) worried that anything I might sing would be reviewed in the papers and perhaps frowned upon, and guess who might hear about it? This had to be the truth, since

I was told that for the three performances the following weekend, I could sing what I liked, as the critics (it was implied) would not be around to take notes.

This was the first time I had ever been censored (Davide roared when I told him), and – as you will witness – really the lines were very mild indeed.

Quella opera celata sott'un gran tendone,
La Fenice è sulla lista, non potrà mancare,
Chi perde in finale, chi non è campione,
E Berlusconi, e Maroni, e la sinistra radicale,
E chi mette l'orologio sopra il polsino,
Chi veste Gucci o Prada, chi vive nel Ticino,
E insieme a loro i giudici del TAR,
E non dimentichiamo tutto l'Harry's Bar,
Chi porta strani piercing, chi vede i Varietà –
Nessuno dalla lista – nessuno mancherà.

(Last line for final performance)
La bomba è sulla lista, nessuno mancherà.

There's the opera company that's hidden under a large tent
The Fenice's on my list, I'm sure it won't be missed.
And all losers in that football final, they're not the champions.

And Berlusconi, and Maroni, and the radical left.
And those who wear their watch over their shirt-sleeve,
And those who wear Gucci or Prada, and those who live in Ticino,
And with them are the legal men, the judges of the TAR,
And let's not forget the whole of Harry's Bar,
And those who have strange piercings, those who watch TV
  Variety shows:
They'll none of them be missed – they'll none of them be missed.

That bomb is on my list, it never would be missed.

The man who wore a wristwatch over his shirt sleeve was Gianni Agnelli, owner of Fiat and regarded as the best dressed man in Italy. Thousands used to wear their watches like that, just to emulate him.

Ticino is the Italian-speaking part of Switzerland, inevitably looked down on by 'proper' Italians as a very boring place to live.

The TAR is an administrative court to which just about every Italian has had to appeal, in order to correct a bureaucratic anomaly – citizens usually win because the TAR does not sentence within its deadline…

And the bomb? Well, our last performance was held up for an hour whilst an old Second World War bomb, recently found on Tronchetto, was defused. A British bomb…

LA LISTA AT PALERMO

The list writer in Palermo enjoyed translating some of Gilbert's original into Italian, but had a few (non-political!) suspects to add himself. In the first verse, as well as autograph hunters, he included stamp collectors, and – how very Italian – those who keep practising their *do re mi* (himself included, no doubt!). Compulsive story tellers too are included amongst those whose demise might happily relieve the executioner's boredom.

> Il boia è nell'imbroglio, non sa chi giustiziar,
> E allor che cosa fa?
> Egli in un mastro apposito ognun fa registrar
> Che ha qualche qualità.
> Chi francobolli o autografi, aver da tutti vuol,
> E chi rompe le scatole col *do, re, mi, fa, sol,*
> Chi in tasca ognor da leggervi un dramma nuovo tien,
> E chi con vecchi aneddoti a importunarvi vien,
> È gente indicatissima, cui può toccar l'onor
> Di dissipare al boia
> La augusta eccelsa noia.

Coro

> Di gente che del boia
> Può dissipar la noia
> La lista è lunga ancor!

A nice ploy here at the beginning of the second verse to get the audience on side is to include mothers-in-law, together with fat old maids in fancy clothes who insist on pestering people. Writers and wearers of pince-nez are on his list, together with nasal hair-pluckers – there's a cry from the heart – and wives who scream at you when you come in late: he reckons he's got a complete list now…

Ci metto anche le suocere che requie non vi dan
Giustizia non vi par?
Le zitellone in fregola che la corte vi fan
Non son da trascurar.
Le signore che scrivono e portano il *pince-nez*
E le vecchie pinzocchere che annasano *rapè*,
Le moglie che la predica vi fanno se vi avvien
Di tornar tardi, in *cimbalis*, più di quanto convien.
Io credo che d'iscrivere nessun dimenticai…
(Che val! Non può giammai ??)

Coro

Che val! Non può giammai
Finire il libro d'or
Del Grande Esecutor!

But for special occasions or exceptional circumstances, he has reserved a few places on his little black list for poets, fortune-tellers and the like – people who embitter his existence – his sword desires to taste their flesh; they must all be beheaded together – yes, now we are getting back to real Italian opera – and remember, this is Palermo!

> Per un caso di penuria, di bisogno eccezional,
> Che potrebbe anche accader…
> Ho serbato in fondo al mastro una rubrica special,
> E sarà il mio libro ner.
> I poeti simbolisti io vi voglio collocar,
> E codini e avveniristi – che, a chi il bello vuol gustar
> Amareggian l'esistenza, – tutti insiem ci devon star!
> *(agli astanti)*
> Ma però se tutto questo non bastasse ancora, poi…
> Del mio mastro a capolista metto…tutti quanti voi!

Coro

> No, no, grazie dell'onor,
> È completo il libro d'or
> Del supremo Esecutor!

The final chorus tells the audience that if they do not think that this is enough, then he'll put them all on his list... very Berlusconi...

SOCIETEITS COMMISSIE DINER
1888
1889
8 MAART

KO-KO IN THE NETHERLANDS

One cold February morning in 2004, I left Gatwick for Schiphol, and then on by train east to Enschede, home of the Dutch touring opera company, The Nationale Reisopera. I had sung for them on two previous occasions – in *Reigen* (by Philippe Boesmans) and in *Peter Grimes* – when Louwrens Langevoort was Intendant; but now Guus Mostart was at the helm. Previously he had been at English National Opera: there he witnessed *The Mikado*, and he now wanted his company to do it, but with a Dutch creative team (director and designers). Most of the singers would be English with the notable exceptions of the Pish-Tush and Peep-Bo, who were Dutch but had brilliant English, as so many have. We used surtitles, but in many cities I felt these were not needed. A colourful new production emerged, and I let it be known that I would like to do a verse of the list in Dutch: I was happy, I reasoned, with French and German… Surely Dutch would not be too difficult to master?

How wrong I was. I think it is fair to say that Dutch is not a beautiful language to sing in, there are too many gutturals and some very interesting diphthongs – and sometimes it sounds just wrong. We were discussing this during a break on one occasion, and our director offered us the first two lines of *Jesus Christ Superstar* (at full voice), by way of agreement:

> Jezus, mijn superheld
> Ben jij de leider die werd voorspeld.

Opposite: a Dutch fan of 1889. It appears to commemorate a social club dinner – all men, including the maids

Nevertheless I was still game for it and, after all, there was no shortage of coaching. I chanced upon a confident writer too, one Ben Coelman, the most enthusiastic Public Relations manager and G&S fan ever to grace a Dutch company. His flawless English had been perfected on many walking trips to Britain – the Dutch being somewhat short of hills – and we would happily talk of shared experiences in the Peak District and the like. He understood the idiom, and offered me great encouragement, as well as some tongue-twisting lines. Hester Steijn, the wondrous assistant stage manager, was my uncompromising coach. Here, then, are the first four lines:

> De topman die na wanbeleid een gouden handdruk krijgt,
> Let wel, belastingvrij, die schrijf ik er graag bij.
> Het meisje dat in Idols zich door slechte popsongs hijgt,
> Voor haar is volgens mij, nog wel een plekje vrij.

Believe me, they are every bit as tricky as they look! They tell the familiar tale of a top manager of a large company who had been relieved of his duties for irregular practices, but had been let go with a large tax-free sum… Pop-Idol had hit Holland too, and, as Ko-Ko lamented, for the second season on the trot some poor girl was panting her way through another bad song.

Audiences were generous, as were my colleagues, and since the production as a whole was well-received (and because the Arts Council of

The Netherlands stipulates that the Company should do at least one operetta a year) Guus asked us back for more in late 2006. Ben continued to be similarly inspired and, detecting that I was getting happier with Dutch, now started to offer me new lines on the days of performances. I began to dread my phone ringing around coffee time, for invariably it would be Mr. Coelman with another gem or two and a wonderfully infectious giggle. One could never say no.

As for subject matter, the format was much the same as for London. One could use a royal story:

> En de kroonprins gaf down-under de locale pers een knauw,
> Alweer 'een beetje dom', schrijf hem erbij kortom!

Their crown-prince on a recent tour to Australia had been a somewhat rude to the local press, which prompted his wife to label him 'a little stupid'.

Or one could stick to political stories, of which – since it was election time in Holland – there was fortunately no shortage.

> De premier die van een skateboard valt om populair te zijn,
> De partij die stemrecht wil voor goudvis, hamster en konijn.

Prime Minister Balkenende, on one of his promotional tours, 'hung out' with a group of youngsters and gave a skateboard a try... Of course he obligingly fell off right in front of all the TV cameras, enabling the

entire country to witness the event. A new party was born too, one that only concerned itself with animals' rights issues, here illustrated by 'goldfish, hamster and rabbit'.

Celebrities would not let us down either. A young, slightly chubby, Dutch ballad-singer called Jan Smit decided to branch out into designing underwear and swimming costumes, with a nationwide publicity campaign in which he himself appeared on rather larger-than-life posters. Ben was convinced that the photos had been doctored to make him look slimmer than he really was, and thoroughly enjoyed digging out websites to show me the singer's true girth.

> De zanger die een onderbroek van C & A aan wou,
> Als sekssymbool dacht hij, het hoeft niet echt voor mij.

He became quite apoplectic when discussing size, and a soap star's cleavage was the next subject for inclusion (I think I had something similar to say about a certain Osbourne):

> En Georgina met haar Harry's, zijn die nu wel echt of niet,
> Eerst veel te groot en nu te klein, 't is steeds wat met die griet

Harry's is the key word here!

> And Georgina with her knockers, are they real or are they not,
> First way too large and now too small, this item is still hot.

Naturally, I applaud the Dutch for taking to *The Mikado*, and rumour has it that we shall be back for more. I only hope that Ben has not moved on by then.

And yes, they did keep the surtitles for my verse each night… in Dutch. I had suggested Japanese, but was over-ruled!

SOME GENERAL VICTIMS

It is the unhappy lot of any compilation of this nature that certain topics refuse to be neatly categorised. This has not, of course, prevented us from including them here, in a section which might as well have been entitled 'other folk in whose demise Ko-Ko would feel a high (but perfectly justified) level of Schadenfreude'. For instance…

All those who drive along the middle of our motorways,
Causing jams on the M25 that last for days and days.
And those who let their dogs in parks and pavements make a mess,
There's a case to get the pooper-scooper on the NHS.

All those who clutter phone boxes with small ads by the score,
Offering bondage, whipping, therapy – and quite a handful more.

And Marks & Spencer's queues which now want five items or less –
With a basic grasp of English, fewer would be less a mess.

There's all those BT adverts claiming – it's good to talk;
And those who use the pavements more to cycle, not to walk.

And those burly lads who're after all just doing what they ought –
The West End wheel-clampists – they'll soon be on your list!

There are those who take their hols in *gîtes* and think it rather chic
To drive at over 90 in their *Vorsprung durch Technik.*

Opposite: John Reed

Darrell Fancourt as the Mikado, a role he performed over 3,000 times

When I began compiling my lists, the City was shedding jobs:

> There's the Yuppy with his Filofax and golden Amex card –
> No – that's Morgan Grenfell's list! Well, he's also on MY list.
>
> All those who spend their days watching financial indices,
> All admen, conmen, vat-men and Jehovah's witnesses.

And Arthur Scargill was hanging on to the miners, as well as his hair, but dark rumours were circulating about the origins of his funding…

> … the leader of the NUM who needs a new toupee,
> That's fine, he gets his mortgage paid by Colonel Gaddafi.

As so often, the magic is in the accent.

In the early '90s, private companies were getting themselves into all manner of difficulties. A vacuum-cleaner manufacturer was caught out using a dubious ad campaign to encourage us to buy more of their products:

> Those promotions men at Hoover who've been vacuumed by
> the press:
> Those free flights don't exist! – I'll cross them off my list.

and the movement of prisoners around the country had been privatised with alarming results:

> There's those friendly men who set free all our prisoners in
> distress –
> The Group Four escortists – I've got them on my list.

The Ministry of Defence found itself defenceless against some pretty tough opposition in 1994:

> ... those mums who sued the MoD in manner monetarist,
> Post-coital feminists – they never would be missed.

... reminding me of a favourite pair from the very early nineties:

> Now sexual harassment has produced great tales of woe,
> But none as great as those from us whose wives can now say
> "No".

From too little sex, to too much, of course:

> And all those randy teenagers whose kissing knows no bounds,
> The meningococcal virus is enjoying doing the rounds.

The MoD wasn't the only embattled institution in these troubled times:

> And our postal system's name in which nobody does delight,
> Consignia's on my list, I know that won't be missed.

Another success for the Curse of Ko-Ko's Little List. I feel proud.

Sir Henry Lytton, himself on occasion a Mikado, frequently appeared as Ko-Ko opposite Darrell Fancourt

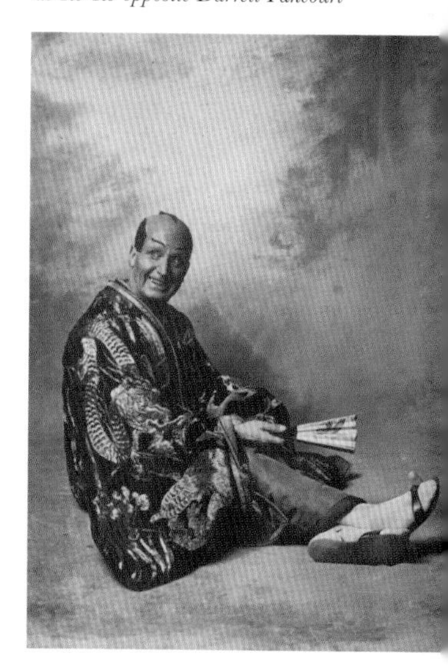

And those silly striking postmen who compel us all to fax
And Skodas, Ladas, Lloyd Webbers, and men who jog in slacks.

As the decade wore on, Ko-Ko saw no reason to believe that he'd run out of victims any time soon.

All those who dumb-down TV – yes, it's rubbish through
the night –
And men who talk in RAM and ROM and no doubt megabyte.

There's those dodgy scientists who want to tamper with our
food –
Modified geneticists – I've them on list my got.

And all those millionaires, for whom to speculate is good –
The nerdy dot-commists – I've got them on my list.

The new millennium year offered an unmissable target:

And those who think the Dome should be knocked down a.s.a.p,
Including those who force an entry on a JCB.

And various other modern fads got Ko-Ko's goat;

All those who piercing rings in awkward places can't resist –
Just what happens when they kiss? I'll give that girl a
miss.

And the scourge of all pedestrians, the micro-scooterist,
I don't think he'll be missed.

Inclusivity, of course, is all:

There are those who stare at snooker, football, cricket – also darts
The couch-potatoists – we're all upon the list.

And for those of you alert enough to spot this Ko-Ko's roots:

Bank managers, accountants, politicians and that sort,
And those who think that Blackpool really is a nice resort.

Occasionally, an intellectual of some sort over-steps the mark, much to the ex-tailor's delight:

There's that teacher come from Canada, a keen biologist,
I've got her on my list – she's top of Ko-Ko's list!

Everyone likes to see a multinational brought low, and the launch of a 'brand new' bottled water could hardly have been more troubled:

There's that company which on bottling Sidcup water does insist,
Ko-Ko-Cola's on my list – reverse osmosisist.

I loved this story, as any of you who know Sidcup would – especially that famous Pinter tramp…

Telephones – and the communications we seem fated to receive via them – I find very disturbing:

> Phone numbers that you press for many different kinds of
> reasons,
> Then wait on hold forever with Vivaldi's *The Four Seasons.*
>
> And those people phoning up at night when you're watching
> the telly,
> Offering double glazing, which is strange, when they're calling
> from Delhi.

The blame ought not to lie with the technology, *per se*, but rather with the young, the old, the single and the married: anyone, in fact, who uses the infernal devices to make everyone else's lives a misery…

> … those whose Christmas letters are just me, me, me and mine,
> The round robin egotists – they'd none of 'em be missed.

Leading (in a strong field), the sight that now greets us everywhere:

> … that great communicator, yes, I think you get the gist.
> The nodding iPodist – I don't think he'd be missed.

CONTEMPLATION (MEMO TO THE GENERAL MANAGER OF THE FAMILY HEALTH SERVICES AUTHORITY)

Here's a fun medical one, written by Dr Marie Campkin and published in her book *The GP's Songbook* in 1995 – I think we can all sympathise…

As one day it may happen that our work needs sorting out,
We've got our practice list, we're looking through the list
At some surgery attenders who we well could do without,
And who never would be missed they never would be missed.
There's the seventeen-stone girl who swears she eats 'just like
a bird,'
The aerophagic dowager whose plaint is loudly heard.
All anorexic virgins with their dietary quirks,
And all the costive matrons whose digestion never works;
And the hooligans who burst into your office when they're pi….
They'd none of them be missed – they'd none of them
be missed.

Chorus He'll take them *off* the list etc.

There's the hobnail-livered veteran who 'hardly takes a drop,'
And the whole-food herbalist – I'll take him off my list.
The neurotics, whose recitals, like their bowels, never stop,
They never would be missed – they never would be missed.
Then the corpulent executive with apoplectic face,
Whose ulcer, gout and gallstones all compete for pride of place.

And the child who 'never eats' but still has strength to wreck
your room,
Whose mother's haggard face portrays anxiety and gloom.
While his father keeps demanding he should see a specialist,
I don't think he'd be missed – I'm sure he'd not be missed.

Chorus He'll take them off the list etc.

The Community Health Counsellor who's touting for complaints,
And the 'social scientist' – I'll have them off the list.
The addicts whose deceits would try the patience of the saints,
They'd none of them be missed – they'd none of them be
missed.
There's the garrulous earth-mother with her irritating tricks,
Such as booking one appointment for her family of six.
Then when you think that finally you've got her to the door,
She says 'Oh Doctor, while I'm here, I'll just ask one thing more.
Then she has to get undressed to show some small sebaceous
cyst,
She'd surely not be missed – she'd surely not be missed.

Chorus And it really doesn't matter who gets taken off the list,
For they'd none of them be missed – they'd none of them be
missed.

ROYALS

In the late eighties and early nineties, royal-watchers had a field day – there were affairs, divorces and a parade of lovers. Sarah Ferguson provided excellent examples:

> And that Duchess whose financial acumen has known no bounds,
> The big toe fetishist, Weight Watchers on my list.

While photos did the rounds of an older, balding, American accountant sucking her toes, Sarah busied herself writing books on helicopters…

> There's the Grand Old Duke of York who's known to like a
> fine bikini.
> His wife prefers a Budgie, now what hope for their Eugenie?

Of course it was Princess Diana who offered most, in all ways.

> There's that Jamie with his carphone – what a tender, racing man.
> How silly he should use it within yards of Sandringham!
>
> Now Mills & Boon is quite all right for just a quick flick through it,
> But not one that seeks to glorify that bounder Major Hewitt.
>
> Princess Di has said the naked shots of Charles did not affect her.
> Just imagine seeing again those radiant orbs and that old sceptre!
>
> There's that dear Princess who's dearer now by 17 million pounds,
> The regal divorcist; her mother's been quite pi….

Opposite: The town of Titipu in the 1938 film

Just occasionally, though, Ko-Ko hinted at a (deeply-buried) social conscience:

> And those mediocre journalists who write in prying manner,
> Just to make a mint of money from defenceless, poor Diana.

And so to the third person in the marriage:

> Now Parker-Knolls are said to be quite comfortable to lie on –
> Most mistresses are well-sprung, not a shoulder just to cry on:
>
> Yes, that regal anti-disestablishmentarianist,
> Camilla's on my list, I'm sure she'd not be missed.

The Queen helped Ko-Ko sum it up best:

> The royals had a bad year, but their Latin caught the gist:
> Annus horribilis – I'm sure it won't be missed.

A lot changed with the untimely death of Diana, and royal victims were not included for some years; but as they emerged from adolescence the young princes began to offer opportunities:

> There's that Prince who likes a drop of booze and maybe too
> a smoke,
> The Highgrove cannabist, I've got him on my list.

Guarding the Royal family has always been a time-consuming affair. Still, one might think that the long and unsocial hours spent at the various palaces and castles would make those entrusted with the task somewhat wary of surveillance…

> And that close-to-bursting police chief caught against the palace walls,
> By a closed-circuit TV that showed a close-up of his balls.

I was at a dinner in a very smart hotel in Lausanne once where I found myself sitting next to Princess Diana's former bodyguard. We chatted in a very relaxed manner and I commented that I bet he had some stories to tell; he became reticent, and I put this down to professional etiquette. The photographer at the event took a snapshot of the two of us chatting, and I was quite proud of it until I realised that some months later the bodyguard was the one to write his own book and spill the beans on his late employer – not etiquette, just greed. But then the royal butler had already infamously set the trend:

> And those who profit greatly from their stories up for sale:
> The butler's on my list – he never would be missed.

And indeed, I do not think he is at all.

Mr.Suart, we are not amused !
Olly

THE MIKADO
A Scene in Koko's Garden
SEE "THE SPHERE" FOR GILBERT AND SULLIVAN
OPERA PICTURES - ONE SHILLING WEEKLY

THE NATIONAL TRUST LITTLE LIST

This Little List was written by Philip Walsh especially for a show he created – *Savoyard Express*, based on the D'Oyly Carte touring in the 1890s by train. His society – St. Leonard's Gilbert and Sullivan Group, based in Penwortham, near Preston – took it to several places (including the Buxton G & S Festival) and on each occasion Philip re-wrote the script to suit the venue.

The version here was written for the Ribble Centre of the National Trust, which provides stewards for Trust properties. It was performed 'only once' at Barton Village Hall, near Preston. Philip gives us four verses – evidently, there are just too many offenders among us visitors for the traditional three to be sufficient!

As some day it may happen that a victim must be found,
I've got a little list – I've got a little list,
Of National Trust offenders who might well be underground
And who never would be missed, they never would be missed.
There's the pestilential nuisances who touch the tapestries,
And set the bells a-ringing in their search for antiquities.
All children who are up in dates, and think that they know
best,
And just to prove that they are right, pull down the Baron's Crest.
And the manager who interferes, and slaps the occasional wrist,
They'd none of 'em be missed – they'd none of 'em be missed.

Opposite: Souvenir fan from The Sphere, *c. 1920*

There's the walker who ignores the signs that say you 'Must Not
Go'
The path erosionist – I've got him on the list.
And the careless tobacco smoker who discards his fag ends too,
The Forest Arsonist – I've got him on the list.
Then the idiot who lets his dog roam free at lambing time,
To the farmer, it's his livelihood – but to him it's not a crime.
And the hiker who jumps over and dislodges dry stone walls,
And drops his litter in the tarns, in lakes and waterfalls.
And that singular anomaly – the hunting lobbyist,
I don't think he'd be missed, I'm sure he'd not be missed.

There's the youth who writes 'Kilroy was here' upon the
bedroom door,
The wicked humorist – I've got him on the list.
And people with their back packs, push-chairs, and big
hob-nailed boots,
They never would be missed – they never would be missed.
There's the folk who bring their own food in the tea-room
at the rear,
And walk right through the gift-shop without buying a souvenir.
Next the honeymooning couple behind the 'Private' doors
they kissed,

And the alcoholics on the bottle – must be 'Brahms and Liszt,'
And the badge holder who parks for 'nowt' because of his
poor wrist,
I don't think he'd be missed – I'm sure he'll not be missed.

There's the family who on Open Day turn up in their
Rolls Royce,
The rich numismatist – I've got him on the list.
And members who forget their cards and say with weeping voice,
'Don't put us on the list – don't put us on the list.'
Then the lady from the States who with her ancestry's
well-versed,
And bores you with her family names from James to George
the First
And 'st 'st 'st and what's his name, and also Virginia who?
The task of filling up the blanks I'd rather leave to you.
But it really doesn't matter whom you put upon the list,
For they'd none of 'em be missed, they'd none of 'em be missed.

Apart from a whole host of neat and topical gags, it is a relief to see – in the fourth verse – such an overt reminder that featuring on a list (any list) is often emphatically not a desirable thing. As several of Ko-Ko's correspondents have demonstrated, the implications of being on the Little List are not always understood.

LORD COWDREY MEMORIAL LITTLE LIST

One of my most memorable renditions of the Little List was not in a theatre at all, or even a concert hall, but in Westminster Abbey. It was at the Memorial service for that wonderful cricketer Colin Cowdrey, and for the occasion Tim Rice had written the lyrics. He included new words for Ko-Ko's entrance too, which I include here. It was with much pride that I heard the Abbey Choir sing the chorus – 'Defer, defer, to a model English cricketer':

> Behold a cricketer most suitable
> A personage with noble rank and title;
> Whose sportsmanship was indisputable
> Which on and off the field is simply vital.
> Defer, defer to a model English cricketer,
> Defer, defer to a model English cricketer.

Ko-Ko

> Taking guard in Bangalore
> By a set of curious chances,
> I progressed to England's shore
> To the Tonbridge green expanses,
> Where I fashioned many a score
> That attracted Kentish glances;
> And by nineteen fifty-four
> I was taking up my stances,

To the sound of Melbourne's roar,
Leading to some great advances.
After forty years or more
To most noble circumstances.
Taking guard in Bangalore
By a set of curious chances,
After forty years or more
I had fashioned quite a score.

As some day it may happen that a victim must be found
I've got as little list – I've got a little list
Of some cricketing offenders I would banish from the ground
And who never would be missed, they never would be missed.
Such as coaches who would rather run ten miles than hold a net,
And chaps whose innings end because some blighter placed a bet.
I used to think that sledging was a sport that needed snow,
But now I know it's something else, it really has to go.
And how can stretch pyjama cricket trousers still exist?
They'll none of 'em be missed – they'll none of 'em be missed.

There's the deadly spin of Ramadhin, the blazing speed of Wes
So tricky to resist, I've got them on my list.
There's running with Sir Geoffrey and no matter what he says

He's going on the list – young Boycs is on my list.
And then there are selectors who decide the thing to do
Is make you face some blinding pace when you are forty-two;
Or send you out in fading light in plaster head to toe.
And EGMs at MCC – I bid them cheerio!
And the off-the-field sensation-seeking tabloid journalist,
I don't think he'll be missed, I'm sure he won't be missed.

And then there is the batsman who will never walk alas,
I'd slap him on the wrist – I've got him on the list,
Unless at least three stumps have been uprooted from the grass,
I think you get the gist – I've got him on the list.
And sons who think mid-wicket is the only place to aim,
But then perhaps I'm lucky that they loved the greatest game.
And my sweet loquacious daughter who'll be talking even now,
But always made me chuckle so I think I shall allow
My nearest and my dearest to escape my little list
It's a gesture nepotist – I think they would be missed.

It's a gesture nepotist – I think they would be missed
Kate, Robert, Jamie, Julius, Fabian, Charlie, Lucy, Lara, Michael…*
He thinks they would be missed!

* Lord Cowdrey's grandchildren

SPORTSMEN AND WOMEN

Our dozy English cricket team who don't know where
they're at,
They have a lot of trouble in connecting ball and bat.

I am afraid this pair of lines makes regular appearances on the Little List. However, whilst on tour in India one year, the team did much better in one particular Test Match, and an alert percussionist from English National Opera generously relayed the oversight to the radio commentary team in Delhi, resulting in Aggers tearing me off a strip!

The cricketers themselves became controversial during an unrecognised trip to South Africa:

There's those rebel English cricketers who've caused a lot of fuss,
Oh no, that's Nelson's list, well, they're also on my list.

Tennis makes a brief appearance (the show is rarely on in the summer) thanks to the off-the-court difficulties of one of its former lady stars:

There's sweet Martina's friend whose final set was greed and
lust,
The palimonetrist – I've got her on my list.

As you will no doubt have noticed, Ko-Ko reserves the right to tailor words especially to aid rhyme. Palimony was all the rage in assessing who got what in separation cases; but, as is so often the way, Ms

Navratilova's pal was no friend at all at the end…

Even ice-skating glides in for a mention, though attached (as it weren't) to a far more painful incident:

> There's those leggy, lanky ladies, yes, those friendly ice-skatists,
> And that male-dismemberist: Mrs Bobbit's on my list.

Ouch…

Boxing has merited a few couplets over the years. Gentle Frank just got a little too gentle towards the end of his career (prior to panto):

> It's really very passé to drink Beaujolais Nouveau,
> But a damn sight more exciting than a round with Frank Bruno.

And towards the end of his career, Mike Tyson resorted to unconventional tactics – first:

> There's that boxer who enjoyed himself with aural intercourse,
> He should have used his fist, Mr Tyson's on my list.

… and later

> … that boxer with no licence who on biting legs insists,
> Mike Tyson's on my list – his left hook won't be missed.

However, as one might expect in the UK, we can look to football for the richest mentions. To ease us in gradually, we can generalise about

> … those footballers whose manners give us cause for great
> concern,
> Whatever sums they're paid they cannot possibly earn.

Managers started the rot with a certain Englishman in the early nineties:

> And football managers who're great with simple cocktail chat
> Uttering pithy little sayings like 'Do I not likuh that.'

But it didn't take long for players to come into their own.

> There's that rude and belching soccer star who's always in a mess
> The Lazio burpist – I'm sure he'll not be missed.
>
> Or that cerebrally-challenged, soccer-playing wife-beatist,
> The blond peroxidist, I've got him on my list.

Already we see a pattern – that it is often towards the end of a player's career that he starts to make the mistakes (or just the odd glaring error) that merit inclusion, like

> … that Mancunian goal-keeper whose feats are jolly utter,
> With his success he'll soon be advertising Anchor butter.

Pre-season tours are something of a lottery for teams whose members find the lure of the opposite sex just too tempting:

And those Leicester City footballers in trouble down in Spain,
Their team-bonding week-end antics left their ball-skills in some pain.

When it comes to matters foreign, one particular commentator found that turning off the mic is an important lesson:

… that football pundit who got caught not using asterisks,
Old Ron is on my list – that language won't be missed.

I got told off about the rhyme with this next one (just to let you know how narrow-minded the anoraks can be!):

And those footballers who dabble in the torrid world of texts,
If all those tales are truthful, it's the end for Tosh and Becks.

And who was the reason for this?

That daughter of the diplomat – a keen bisexualist;
Double Dutch is on my list – you bet *she*'s on my list.

Groucho Marx with Helen Traubel as Katisha. Photo courtesy of the MacPhail Gilbert and Sullivan Collection

THE CHESSTAPO

This charming Little List appeared in the *British Chess Magazine* in February 1944 and is by F. J. Whitmarsh of Hove, who adds 'with apologies to the shade of W. S. Gilbert'.

Of objectionable persons who infest the realm of Chess
I've got a little list – I've got a little list,
Their premature extinction wouldn't cause acute distress
For they never would be missed, they'd none of 'em be missed.
The spectator whose acquaintance with the game is not profound
And whose *sotto voce* comments are essentially unsound:
The pest who has a tendency (of which but few approve)
To hum or croon or whistle while you wait for him to move,
And looks surprised and injured if you ask him to desist –
I've got 'em on the list, and they never would be missed.

The fiend whose pipe's extremely foul and constantly aglow,
I've got him on the list – I've got him on the list;
His opponents, if asthmatic, make a brief and sorry show,
So of course he's on the list – in fact he heads the list.
The crank agog with details of that match game won by him,
So vague, involved and wordy that your head begins to swim;
The sportsman, who defeated in a most decisive way
Three times in quick succession, growls 'I'm out of form today' –

There seems no valid reason why these fellows should exist;
I've got 'em on the list, and they'd none of them be missed.

The man who wants his move back when outwitted by a trap,
I've got him on the list – I've got him on the list.
And those whose meditations give you time to have a nap
Are likewise on the list, and they never would be missed.
The wretch who bangs his Queen down ('Check!') with fierce,
aggressive air,
And causes every other piece to totter off its square:
And the cocksure mediocrity, impervious to a snub,
Who hints that he can hold his own with any in the club.
(I'd cheerfully decapitate this hardboiled egotist) –
They're all down on the list, and they'd none of 'em be missed.

FRANKIE HOWERD DENNIS PRICE
and STUBBY KAYE
in
THE COOL MIKADO (U)
Written and directed by MICHAEL WINNER
Produced by HAROLD BAIM
Eastman Colour

CELEBRITIES AND THE PRINT MEDIA, SO OFTEN INTERTWINED

The whole concept of celebrity has really become debased during my time as a List-writer – television, and especially reality TV, has a lot to answer for! – and so I am not sure anymore how some people should be described: film-stars, pop-stars, supermodels (I always imagine super-tankers here, but I would be quite wrong)?

Nonetheless, I have a fondness for 'characters' in general, and when it comes to writing the Little List they often prove incredibly useful.

Lord Archer is fairly incorrigible, and even outside of politics manages to appear again

> There's that perjurer and umpire who just gave his team-mate Out!
> Not for two years, I insist – Jeffrey Archer's on my list.

… and again

> There's that party-loving prisoner, having fun in every jail,
> Naughty Jeffrey's on the list – he never would be missed.

The world of film is represented. We recall an English actor ('the lewd-behaviourist') who came to grief in America:

> There's that lady from Los Angeles who's really quite Devine
> That propositionist – I've got her on my list.

and then an American actor who had a spot of bother in a park in south London:

Opposite: Frankie Howerd as Ko-Ko in 1962

And that ac*tor* who taking walks in parks quite late just can't resist
Renowned somnambulist – his dog is on my list.

In the theatrical world an actor is often known as an ac*tor* – especially if he is a famous one – so I make no apology about the stresses in the previous lines; I say this because irate keepers of the word have already complained to me about it, and really life is too short (though, I fear, too long for them).

Bizarre 'Hollywood' weddings have also gained momentum, together with an equally jet-setting approach to acquiring children:

There's celebrities who go to choose their children from abroad
Mrs. Ritchie's on my list – that Madonna won't be missed.

And those whose secret wedding is so hyped that I am bored
The Scientologists – those crews are on my list.

Popular music has offered us some splendid oddities:

There are pop-stars who have stupid names that make you want t
to wince
Such as Blur, Oasis, and The Artist Formerly Known As Prince.

And:

English Heritage is putting up blue plaques for famous popsters
And Dana's up for President – we've all gone off our rockers.

A visit to the Handel House in Brook Street illustrates the remark about English Heritage: if you look up at the building from the street, to admire Handel's memorial, your eye will be taken to the left where you will read that Jimi Hendrix lived next door.

Mick Jagger has always been keen advocate of the 'extended family':

> And finally that aged Rolling Stone philanderist
> Some satisfactionist – I'm sure he'd not be missed.

And where rock-stars lead, supermodels are sure to follow:

> That so-called supermodel who on writing books insists
> She's off the Booker list, but I've got her on *my* list.
>
> And that supermodel who the odd banned substance can't resist
> Anonymous narcotist – Naomi's on my list.

Here's a man I find hard to categorise, though I think he should appear closer to Jeffrey Archer. In the early nineties The *Evening Standard* ran a banner headline about him which read 'Liar, Liar, Liar.' This I think referred to his take-over of Harrods and the allegedly incorrect information he fed to the authorities.

> Department stores have bunks, divans, settees and double-beds,
> But at Harrods the best liar is a set of Al Fayeds.

Plenty of other big-businessmen also made the cut, and not always for such bad reasons. For example,

> That bearded wonder with balloon going slower than a tractor:
> Yes, Branson had to pull out, but his Virgin's still intacta.

Despite his millions, Brits still like to see Sir Richard as the underdog, and enjoy cheering him on when he comes up against more established commercial interests:

> Like that so-called favourite airline that was recently in court
> For being anti-Bransonist – BA is on my list.

In the late eighties, a certain Murdoch press editor ran into trouble when his girl-friend turned out to be not quite who (or indeed what) he thought she was;

> And that Sunday paper editor whose girl-friend Paella
> Was a propositionist – I've got her on my list.

The other press baron at the time was in deeper water;

> There's the Mirror Group's proprietor who's accused of being
> a spy,
> Oh dear, oh dear, it serves him right for suing Private Eye.

That, alas, was only the tip of the iceberg – but here's the Italian version:

And the media-owning mogul whose finances are quite phoney
I don't mean that Australian, but the charming Berlusconi.

More recently a new figure emerged in the newspaper industry:

… that pornographer and donor to the Labour Party coffers,
From Asian Babes to Readers' Wives, and many other offers.

But the final word should go to the Director of Public Prosecutions, a man whose job it is, after all, to keep these shady types in check. A recent incumbent was found to be somewhat flawed, but so too was one in 1990…

Our inter-city trains are slower than the TGV:
At King's Cross nothing's faster than an erring DPP.

I'VE GOT A LITTLE CLONE

Another medical one, this time from the States, created by Tom Shepard:

As some day it may happen that a kidney must be found,
I've got a little clone – I've got a little clone
Of my DNA and RNA and other genes around,
And the marrow of my bone – I've nurtured all alone!
Any time that a replacement part is needed in my bod'
I do not seek some specialist or vainly pray to God.
I just retire to my cave and undo all the locks,
I rummage through my chemicals and check out all my crocks;
And when I am convinced that I have turned up every stone
I pillage from my clone – I pillage from my clone.

Chorus

He pillages his clone, he pillages his clone;
Who by now is fully grown, by now is fully grown.

I needed a left nostril and an eyeball was askew,
A spoiled retinal cone – I took them from my clone.
My neck was awfully wrinkled and my shoulder withered too
I took them from my clone – I swiped them off my clone.
And I know it may seem callous if I hasten to admit
My badly wrinkled phallus was in need of quite a bit;

And my herniated discs were hurting more than I could bear,
And my emphysemic lungs were crying for a breath of air:
But what the hell, thank God I didn't have to weep or moan,
I vandalised my clone, re-sectioned my young clone.

Chorus

Despite his awful drone – and his supercilious tone,
He is grateful to his clone – he really digs his clone.

Pure and healthy soaps –
a cut above the rest?
American trade card c. 1885

I Use

KOKO FOR THE HAIR

Miss ELLEN TERRY, our Great Actress, writes:—

I have used "KOKO" for the Hair for years, and can assure my friends that it stops the Hair from falling out, promotes its growth, eradicates Dandriff, and is the most pleasant dressing imaginable.

See SPECIAL OFFER on this Page.

Prevents Hair Falling.

KOKO FOR THE HAIR

ROYAL TESTIMONIAL.

KEEPS THE HEAD FREE

Berlin
Alsenstrasse
Feb 25th 1896

"Koko" for the hair, is the best dressing I know. It keeps the head cool, promotes growth, and is in every way excellent.

Princess Hohenlohe

FROM SCURF & DANDRIFF.

A Doctor writes:—

Original can be seen at Company's Office. — Gentlemen, — After using your "Koko" for over six months, I must acknowledge its superiority over any other dressing for the hair which I have tried. — It keeps the head perfectly cool, and it *does* eradicate dandriff, and gives the hair a fine, glossy appearance. The medical treatment of dandriff may be summed up in six words—viz., "Keep the head saturated with oil." No doubt this is efficient; but if we adopt this method, the head becomes dirty, for the simple reason that all moving particles are caught and retained by the oil; and again, bed-linen is rendered disgusting by being stained. Now, your "Koko" possesses none of these disadvantages, and is equally, if not more, effectual. It is for this reason that I prefer it to any other dressing. Since first trying it, I have used no other, and have great pleasure in recommending it to my friends and patients. I send you this little note merely to let you know how well pleased I am with your preparation. — I am, yours, &c.

Special Offer to Readers of "HOME CHAT."

COUPON.

A 4/6 TRIAL BOTTLE FOR 2/-.

P E. Any person forwarding this Coupon, and P. O. for Two Shillings, and Five Stamps to pay postage, package, etc., will receive immediately, for trial, by Parcel Post, under cover, prepaid, One regular 12 oz. Bottle of Koko for the Hair, the price of which is 4s. 6d., provided it is ordered within ten days from date of this offer. In no case will more than one bottle be sent for the use of the same person on this Coupon, as we make the offer solely for trial, knowing it creates a demand when once used; and this large bottle gives it a fair trial. We find it better to thus practically give away one bottle to make a customer than to spend large amounts in advertising. Any person into whose hands this offer comes may avail themselves of it. Address all Orders with Coupon to—

KOKO-MARICOPAS CO., LTD., 16 Bevis Marks E. C, London.

Orders may be sent with this Coupon after the expiration of date, providing we are then issuing these Trial Bottle Coupons, and if we are not the money will be returned. This Coupon will be received at 16, Bevis Marks, E. C. or 233, Regent Street, W., and 2s. only will be required when presented personally.

Printed in Bavaria.

TV AND POPULAR CULTURE

Television has always offered rich pickings for Ko-Ko. In the early nineties, the BBC made an attempt to set a new soap in Spain; *Eldorado*, for which they built a load of villas for the set, was mentioned earlier in this book, rhyming happily, as it does, with Mikado. Alas, the buildings lasted longer than the series. But another, based in France, did well:

> French fishermen act dangerously, protesting innocence,
> So why are we so partial to A Year in Mayle's Provence?

A performance or two in December gave rise to:

> And then there's Christmas TV – which is why we're here tonight –
> That's despite our friends at Railtrack (yes, that snow is far too white).

And an irritant that has gone on far too long:

> All fly-on-the-wall TV shows, but by now you've got the gist,
> I mean of course Big Brother which should really not exist.

And here are some more characters who are (amazingly) still around:

> And those fans of Tinky Winky whose behaviour's rather coarse
> The Tellytubbyists – I'm sure they'll not be missed.

Opposite: So why are most Ko-Kos bald?

Unlike

> … those children who have found a substitute for teddy bears,
> The Tamagotchi-ists – they never would be missed.

I rarely seem to include religion, though in 1996 there was

> That bishop who'd been struggling for months not to be kissed –
> The ex-celibacist….

And the year before

> Now actresses and bishops are historically keen –
> Let's add a lady verger and an impish Lincoln Dean.

TV religion however offered the most fun, and in North America there was a spot of trouble in the nineties, featuring

> … those TV screen evangelists who preach from morn till night,
> Who when the camera's off of them bed everything in sight.

This spilt over into Yorkshire (of all places…) with a vicar who was trying to tune in more to his congregation:

> And Sheffield's raving reverend, like TV evangelists,
> With his special service list – it's the nine o'clock I missed.

Well, those were the days, now long past – unlike some people:

... that ginger-haired interrogator with annoying wink,
Goodbye, my dear Anne Robinson, you are the weakest link.

Or that frightening dominatrix who some botox can't resist,
Weakest Link is on my list, I don't think she'd be missed.

However, another show just goes on and on:

And that quiz-show host whose private life has been exposed as grim
The Sunday papers told us, and the Beeb had news for *him*.

Other individuals find themselves included, if for no other reason than being too big for their boots:

There are spinsters writing books and thus disclosing wild affairs,
Just who is this MacGregor? Is there anyone who cares?

There are occasions when a little admiration is mixed with thinly-disguised envy:

And that aged entertainer who to sire just can't resist,
That septuagenarianist, Des O'Connor's on my list.

... but generally the horror and incredulity are quite sincere:

... the Osbournes, too, especially the multi-tasking wife
That cleavage must be missed – I had it on my list.

> Those cosmetic operations on TV are something else,
> It's not the actual surgery, but more Vanessa Feltz.

We have strayed away from the notion of never mentioning names, but let us conclude with

> All those media chefs and hordes of wretched home
>   make-overists –
> I've got them on my list – they'd none of them be missed.

Radio is the poor relation in the Little List ratings, though the former Home Service made it once:

> And those listeners who've complained that Lady Chatterley is
>   not
> A proper book at bedtime when their Horlicks is still hot.

A certain Director General of the BBC made sweeping changes in all areas:

> And those Radio Three DJs attempting all things populist
> Just bimbo-like Birtists – I'm sure he'd not be missed.

And indeed he wasn't, especially considering he was

> … the top man at the BBC, who's taxed as self-employed,
> His secretary's salary no doubt his wife enjoyed.

I fear that owing to Ko-Ko's listening preferences, only one appearance is made by Radio 1, and indeed (rather fittingly, since it is difficult for a radio station to 'appear') this was in conjunction with the TV:

> And that orange-haired and over-paid (though lazy) disc-jockist,
> I think you've got the gist – his Fridays won't be missed.

Theatre gets a mention:

> All those who utter monologues on female body parts,
> I've got them on my list – I'd like to see *their* list…

As does the movie world:

> If nakedness was not a topic for the sisters Bronte,
> What would they make of Yorkshire lads now doing The Full Monty?

Perhaps our last inclusion can sum up the whole chapter:

> There's that winner of the Turner Prize where lights go on and off
> If you blink it will be missed – I've got him on my list.

When Eric Idle first assumed the role of Ko-Ko in Jonathan Miller's production, I understudied him. I admired him greatly: not only did he speak the text well, but his singing was very presentable and he made a great attempt to be part of the opera company.

Two years later, further performances were planned and I was encouraged to cover the role again – no 'comedian' had yet been found, but actors book much later than singers. At very short notice (in desperation, many might say), someone was found, but he could not do all the planned performances owing to prior commitments. As a result, I was to get five shows, one of which was set to coincide with a general change of cast which was subsequently reviewed in the press.

I was now writing my first lists, and for fun included my colleague, 'the ornithologist'. It is always important to keep the male chorus happy in this song as they are actually facing upstage and therefore can (and will) pull faces with impunity. This inclusion they liked, however, and eventually 'he' got to hear of it, and added the reference to his own list – quite rightly I thought.

Though the press was favourable to me, when the next revival was booked I found myself as understudy once more. Informed that the publicity office found it easier to sell the show with a 'name', I pointed out that the five performances I had done were not exactly undersold: indeed public reaction had been a good deal more effusive in its praise.

Such negotiations were always conducted honourably, and we

agreed a cut-off time for the powers that be to find a 'name'. None was ever found and after that (barring one resurgent effort from the publicity folks), the role was mine, it being finally understood that it was the show itself that sold the tickets, and not any given performer.

This scenario, however, was to haunt me throughout my professional association with G&S: the argument routinely being that the original patterman, George Grossmith, was a 'piano entertainer' and not a singer first and foremost. I would continually point out that singers have come rather a long way since those days, and our training and achievements are greater. Besides which, employing singers does more justice to the music of Sullivan (as any singer will attest who has tried a trio with two actors).

They say that one should never bite the hand that feeds one, but in some cases it is just too tempting, and so, over the years, ENO has come in for its own fair share of criticism in the Little List.

As in any company, complaints are for the most part directed at the upper echelons. Successive boards and managements have made some incredible decisions as to the future of the company. Matters came to a head with the prospect of closure for refurbishment:

> The plight of English National Opera is getting worse here
> So the Board wants in its wisdom to move southwards to
> Battersea

Closure could have meant relocation to an out-of-West End site (never to return, it was assumed), or the building of a temporary theatre near to Tower Bridge. Whatever the outcome, the Board was not popular.

> And the ENO Board who moving from the Coliseum insist
> I've got them on my list – I don't think they'd be missed.

As I delivered these lines, Pooh-Bah turned round to me with a very hurt expression; I had forgotten that the splendid Richard Van Allan was a Board member! So I quickly appeased him;

> ... those critics who've been claiming ENO is in a mess –
> The whingeing journalists – *Evening Standard*'s on my list.

In an attempt to repeat the success of *The Mikado*, the management asked Ken Russell to direct *Princess Ida*. Thirty shows were planned; I was to do a few with an actor doing the lion's share (again!). It seemed we were back to square one. But actually I was fortunate; the rehearsal period had been unhappy and the resulting production was a shambles:

> That director who tried hard to reconstruct a G&S
> That sixties excessist – dear Ken is on my list.

General Directors have come and gone over the life of the production, including one who openly stated in an interview that he really had no

WHY DIDN'T I WIN THE LAURENCE OLIVIER AWARD?

time for G&S. Tragically, he lasted but a short while.

> There's that English National Opera's past General Director
> I had him on my list – I'm sure he'll not be missed.

It was during his tenancy that an edict went out from on high to all members of the company about respect in the workplace…

> All those who using friendly terms like 'darling' can't resist
> Oh no! That's ENO's list – they'd none of them be missed.

Conductors have come and gone, too: one of them was surprised one night to find himself included in Ko-Ko's musings

> … conductors who on leaving out the overture insist

having ditched the overture as being 'not entirely by Sullivan' – authenticity taken to extremes, one felt.

The audience agreed with me. And they did so again when, rather curiously, Covent Garden was offered an Olivier Award for a production that was borrowed from elsewhere:

> And the Olivier Awards which Covent Garden they did win –
> They can't do opera on their own, they buy it from Berlin.

More recently, surtitles have been introduced, though not in the dialogue (thank goodness!) and certainly not for the Little List, which is often still in gestation during the overture.

Still, they manage to antagonise a fair few people:

> And that trendy thing in op'ra just to help you get the gist
> The damned surtitlist – I don't think he'll be missed.

There is always some representative of the management present at ENO performances. Many of the managerial staff are known to performers, but some are not, especially to guest artists like myself. They always come and introduce themselves to us in our dressing rooms during the half-hour before curtain-up. One evening there was a very sheepish knock at the door and a girl came in and rather diffidently let me know that not only was she the management presence for the performance but that she was also the surtitlist. To which I could only point out that I had no problem with the messenger, just the decision.

The Board have often managed to wrangle amongst themselves, too. On one occasion an unpopular Chairman was ousted, to roars of approval from company and audience alike (so important to keep both parties onside).

And the ENO Board who had their knickers in a twist
The Chair was on my list – I don't think he'll be missed.

Not all gaffes emanate from the Board-room. For a recent revival, the marketing department published a brochure that had a facial image for each of the productions featured in the Spring season (i.e. nothing from the show itself – too obvious and insufficiently 'arty') and *The Mikado* was given the beautiful face of a young Japanese girl.

… our marketing department who just don't know where they're at
The brochure for this opera was dreamt up by a prat.

If there's one thing everyone can agree on it is that Jonathan Miller's production has made the show's humour the absolute priority; the publicists would have done well to remember GK Chesterton's remark:

'I doubt if there is a single joke in the whole play that fits the Japanese; but all the jokes in the play fit the English.'

It is true to say that not all revivals of *The Mikado* are planned that far ahead – some are put in when other projects have gone astray. Regulars at ENO will remember *Gaddafi*… An 'opera' which eventually made it to the stage (but is perhaps best forgotten), it should have appeared 6 months previously, and at a time when London buses were being hopelessly reorganised

And those who dumped the Routemaster, an icon of our nation,
And you who'd thought you'd come to hear the Asian
Dub Foundation.

The greatest credit that I can give to the ENO management is that they have never seriously sought to censor me (that dubious honour held, of course, by the Italians). I did once get a discreet telephone call from the press department, informing me that the MP who had recently had an affair with an actress (one of the two was a great Chelsea fan) had just been appointed to the Board – might I consider a re-write? Well, tough one here; but I knew my audience…

Punch's view of D'Oyly Carte

AN OPERATIC LIST

This list, which is reprinted with the kind permission of the author, Tim Hopkins, appeared in a book called *How to be tremendously tuned in to Opera*, edited by E. O. Parrott. It does not quite follow Gilbert's pattern, and was originally printed as a single verse; but in every other respect it is true to the spirit and style of the original.

As some day it may happen that a victim must be found,
I've got a little list – I've got a little list,
Of egregious opera-goers who might well be underground,
And who never would be missed – who never would be missed.
There's the scholar with his pocket-torch-illuminated score,
The parvenu who thinks his cash confers the right to jaw;
All ladies who, *de rigueur*, use their programme as a fan,
The 'modern' girls in ghastly clothes who think they're in a van;
All men who laugh too loud and long at esoteric jokes,
Incipient consumptives with their wheezes, coughs and chokes;

There's the millionaire from Texas with his awful wife and son,
Whose neck you'd like to twist – I've got him on the list.
And the noisy late arrivals pushing past you in Act One,
They never would be missed – they never would be missed.
There's the ostentatious critic who leaves halfway through
  Act Two,
Who cannot sing a note himself yet damns the ones who do;

The man behind informing you of what will happen next,
Who sighs aloud his pique at small excisions from the text;
And the fidget shifting endlessly from left to right and back,
Who during quieter moments likes to hear his knuckles crack.

And the fop who *sotto voce* tries to play the humorist,
I know he'd not be missed – I know he'd not be missed.
The 'Encore!' – yelling arriviste, that brash self publicist
All cheerers, weepers, booers, they'd none of them be missed.
And the teachers with their students, in decorum quite inept,
Who fail to check their charges by example or precept,
But it really doesn't matter who you put upon the list,
They'd none of them be missed – they'd none of them be missed.

OTHER MUSICAL IRRITANTS

There's musicians who insist they play with authenticity,
Those down-a-semi-tonalists, I've got them on my list.
At last we're at the end of Wolfgang's bicentenary
Poor cosi-fan-tuttists – they never would be missed.

It seems only fair that one should include other branches of the musical profession (indeed one maintains the spirit of the original by including oneself in a covert way). In 1991, I had had enough of the Mozart hype for a while, and a few years later it was Purcell's turm:

At last we're at the end of Purcell's tercentenary,
Fairy Queens are on my list – they never would be missed.

Around that time a certain young violinist went off the rails a bit

And Aston Villa's answer to the karaoke-ist,
That punk violinist – I'm sure he'd not be missed.

Classic FM was in its infancy too

And that singular anomaly, the Classic FM-ist
With the errors that persist, I'm sure they won't be missed.

It wasn't just the newcomers to the classical scene who had problems, either. At the Proms, for instance

There's that little band of booers who loathe all things modernist –
Those petty hecklerists – I've got them on my list.

Sir Cliff Richard dazzled us in a new musical

> And those who think that *Heathcliffe* is a show beyond compare,
> And some who said they liked new rehash of *Martin Guerre*.

After my difficulties in securing Ko-Ko at ENO, I had the same humiliation in 2000 at the hands of the D'Oyly Carte (even though my association with them dated back to 1988). A new production of *The Mikado* was proposed at the Savoy, to be directed by Ian Judge and cast, ultimately, by Raymond Gubbay. Once again, there was no 'star' in sight a month before rehearsals were due to begin.

> And all commercial managements who want to cast a star,
> They couldn't find one this time, so they're lumbered with Suart.*

These lines were delivered in rehearsal only, again largely for the benefit of the male chorus. When the Savoy came to put on the revival, however, both Ian Judge and I were dropped, prompting me to write some lines for the Buxton G&S Festival production that year:

> And all those take-aways that make you feel sick as a parrot,
> And dumbed-down D'Oyly Carte whose Ko-Ko now is just a Carrot.

The venues themselves can cause trouble. In 2002 the management of the Buxton jamboree – the enterprising father and son team of Ian and Neil

* French pronounciation helps.

Smith – attempted to broaden the appeal of the Festival by undertaking two weeks in Eastbourne first. On one occasion the theatre fire alarm was a little oversensitive, and we all found ourselves out on the pavement (in full make-up) waiting for clearance from the fire brigade to re-enter and continue with the show. When we finally got back inside, the male chorus began well with

> If you want to know who we are,
> We are firemen from Japan.

And I did my best to continue in the same vein

> And what of new technology that's meant to keep us calm,
> In particular this splendid theatre's dodgy fire alarm?

Celebrity status has been afforded to some on the fringes of our profession. Ko-Ko has little time for the likes of

> … that singular anomaly, the teenage vocalist:
> Charlotte Church is on my list, her *Habanera* won't be missed.
>
> Or that Tenor who appears to be on top of all the charts,
> The Voice is on my list – I don't think he'd be missed.

Then, of course, there is always the cheapening matter of money. I worked for some years for the incomparable Kent Opera – a splendid company founded by Norman Platt – until they were inexplicably axed by the Arts Council in the late 1980s. Their work had been groundbreaking and their standards impeccable, but it turned out that other criteria were being employed in the decision to shut them down.

> … that wretched music panel which did practice gross incest
> For those who killed Kent Opera had a vested interest.

Since one is disenfranchised by the absence of voting in the arts, one hits out occasionally, not least at

> … those ministers who like to cancel grants of any kind –
> If culture disappeared for good I'm sure they'd never mind.

Sadly, such bean-counting is not exclusive to the public sector. One finds similar behaviour from within one's own profession (where people really ought to know better):

> There's that millionaire who's trying to reduce his size of band–
> The Miserable-ist – oh yes, Cameron's on my list.
> And the other offering opera shows just further down the
> Strand –
> Raymondreviewbarist – I don't think he'd be missed.

Yes indeed, occasionally one's own prejudices get the better of one!

THEY NEVER WILL B. MUS

In 1970, the Incorporated Society of Musicians issued a fund-raising LP, entitled *Why was Lloyd George born so beautiful?* It contained three musically intellectual parodies performed by a small choir including Peter Pears and John Carol Case, one of which was Philip Cranmer's 'They never will B. Mus.' (Bachelor of Music). I reprint it here with the kind permission of Philip's son Damian.

In musical departments there will always be a few
Who are not the likes of us, they're not the likes of us.
And whose technical shortcomings make it evident to you
They never will B. Mus., they never will B. Mus.,
There's the pianist who practices with doors all open wide,
The soprano with arpeggios that no one can abide;
The girl that thinks that Massenet is greater far than Bach,
And the man who thinks it must be William Byrd who wrote
The Lark;
And the girl who spends her lectures in the arms of Morpheus,
She never will B. Mus., she never will B. Mus.

The funny man whose answers in exams are frivolous,
He never will B. Mus., he never will B. Mus.,
And the lounger whose philosophy is that of Bertrand Russ-
Ell never will B. Mus., he never will B. Mus.,

And the girl who writes consecutives in all her Bach Chorales,
And the lout who parks his chewing-gum on periodicals;
And the man who thinks that Water Music comes from Noyes Fludde,
With the notion that the Flower Song is sung by Billy Budd;
And the lazy tyke whose average of marks is gamma plus,
He never will B. Mus., he never will B. Mus.

There's the man who can't be bothered playing anything but golf,
He never will B. Mus., he never will B. Mus.,
And the girl who thinks that Nono is the way to stop a wolf,
She never will B. Mus., she never will B. Mus.
There's the man who learnt his counterpoint from Ebenezer Prout,
And the avant-garde enthusiast who's such a long way out.
And the Stainer and the Barnby and the Kitson harmonists,
And disciples of Stockhausen and the total serialists,
And conductors who'd be better off conducting on a bus,
For they never will B. Mus., they never will B. Mus.

Chorus

Though they make a lot of fuss, yet they're not the likes of us,
And they'll none of them B. Mus., they'll none of them B. Mus.

DEAR SIR

Of course, not everyone agrees with the style or (more frequently) the content of every Little List.

> 'We wish to protest in the very strongest terms... The substitute lines were clumsy – worse than anything Gilbert ever wrote – and do not fit into the scheme of the song. But the choice of subject matter is the true offence. Mutilation and misery are repugnant subjects for cheap jokes. The Jackson reference is particularly offensive. Child abuse is never a subject for lowest-common-denominator laughter...'

So wrote a distressed harridan from Hampshire, with copies to Dennis Marks, the General Manager of ENO and Lord Harewood, Chairman of the Board. The offending lines? Well, you may recognise them:

> There's those leggy Yankee ladies, yes, those friendly ice-skatists
> And that male dismemberist, Mrs. Bobbit's on my list.

There were a couple of world-class ice-skaters who were crossing one another's paths a little too literally, whilst many of you will remember what Mrs. Bobbit did to her erring husband (satire, unfortunately, is rarely without bite).

> And that agency that chases dads and slaps them on the wrist
> Those child protectionists, they never would be missed.

In the light of subsequent events, I rest my case as far as the Child Protection Agency is concerned.

A certain former member of the Jackson Five attempted marriage and fatherhood for the first time. His union with Lisa Marie Presley, daughter of Elvis, was not a successful one, especially in the light of certain rumours abounding, which more recently became the subject of two court cases (the Curse of the Little List strikes again…).

> When asked about a family Ms Presley's not been coy,
> But her husband has been heard to say he'd like to have a boy.

Dennis wrote wonderfully in my defence that 'compared to the comments of panellists on the News Quiz at lunchtime on Saturday, [my] satire was mild indeed.' I took a time to prepare my defence and replied at length. To give the lady her credit, she responded;

> 'Your generous letter has just arrived. What a nice man you must be after all. Pardon me for my astonishment. I was aware when I wrote my letter to the ENO that I must inevitably sound like a seven-foot dowager in full battle-dress (no sense of humour implied).'

Indeed, and none inferred, either!

Such letters are few, and inevitably one will upset people – but the essential thing to remember is that the list is fun. Curiously enough, though, when one sees some lines on the written page they do become rather more biting (so, dear reader, if anything offends, just sing it to yourself and all will be well. Bear in mind, too, that these lines were meant to be heard, not scrutinised).

By way of balancing the difficult letters, I occasionally get asked to include people. I particularly enjoyed receiving one such request, from the editor of *The Lady*. He pointed out that the first issue of this family magazine was published in February 1885, only a month before *The Mikado* had its first performances just over the Strand:

Cartoon of 1890, from the Illustrated Sporting and Dramatic News

> *The Mikado* and *The Lady* are thus almost exactly the same age (and equally indestructible, so it would seem), and as we are once again close neighbours after 115 years I am emboldened to ask whether you might possibly consider including at next Thursday's matinee performance 'The Lady Journalist'.

He had booked a couple of rows for his staff Christmas theatre outing at the Savoy, and as he had addressed me as 'Most Respected Sir' it was my pleasure to oblige. Not so, however, with British Gas, who one evening had booked several rows in the Dress Circle at the Coliseum; some things are beyond a joke.

Occasionally, I get requests for a copy of my Little List for a particular evening, and I am very happy to oblige – though I did feel the Judge who wrote to me from the Houses of Parliament jolly well ought to write his own after-dinner speeches!

And, in a curious reversal, I was once sent a list, by a correspondent who felt mine was inadequate. His, it quickly transpired, was unspeakable; be grateful, Dear Dowager, that I have saved you from that.

GRATEFUL THANKS

In preparing this book, I have been quite overwhelmed by the interest and support of many branches of the Gilbert and Sullivan 'family'; whilst searching for original lists, I have made new friendships, and discovered connections that hitherto I did not know existed. Thank you therefore to all of my guest List writers who have so generously allowed me to include their work. I have principally been helped by John Cannon, who possesses more versions of the List than anyone I know, together with countless illustrations; he has been a source of great advice and encouragement, and tireless in his efforts to assist - I thank him most sincerely. Stephen Turnbull of the Sir Arthur Sullivan Society has pointed me in many good directions, and I am most grateful to Olly Burton for his cartoons. Sue Parmenter has kindly given me permission to use her cartoon, which was originally drawn for Sarah Walker, my Katisha at the time. Peter Joslin has generously allowed me to use the delightful 'People who never would be missed' booklet from his magnificent collection; Melvyn Tarran, another avid collector, has an absolutely fascinating G&S collection in Oak Hall Manor close by Sheffield Park Gardens in East Sussex, and I must thank him for the loan of two illustrations as well as an absorbing and instructive morning under his patient, enthusiastic guidance. Many photographers have allowed me to use their work and I would particularly thank Billy Rafferty and Bill Cooper for many of the ENO shots and Jurjen Stekelenburg for the Dutch photo; David Warner Ellis alas died three years ago, but I am

Opposite: We are infinitely obliged to Your Majesty

indebted to his widow Maggie for allowing me to use some of his work. Thank you too to Nicholas Garland for permission to use his cartoon, and to Hester Steijn for her help and knowledge in preparing the Dutch and German chapters. Sir Arthur Sullivan's original score of *The Mikado* is housed at the Royal Academy of Music and I must thank Jo and Kathy in the Library for their help in copying the pages you see.

English National Opera naturally features heavily in this modest volume; it is an organisation that has changed much over the years, not always for the better, but at its best, I find that those who work there are united in their desire to continue the tradition of Opera in English for everybody; G&S fits the bill here pretty well, and together with the many stage managers, technicians, press and marketing men, dressers and make-up artists who have helped me over the years, I would like to thank Anthony McNeill who got me writing in the first place. Great thanks too are due to Emily Stubbs in the Development department for her invaluable help, not only in finding a publisher for my 'idea', but for her support and input.

The identity of my co-writer should no longer be kept a mystery. A fan of the Miller *Mikado* from a worryingly tender age, A(dam) S. H. Smyth had already sung the role of Nanki-Poo at a local girls' school when, in 1998 he talked me out of some work experience. Matters went from bad to worse when he turned Bass, took a choral scholarship at the other university, and became a frequent soloist with the Oxford G&S

Society. In the spring of 2006, Adam knocked on my door, wondered aloud about my archive of Little Lists, and proceeded to flatter me into this literary collaboration. I didn't have the heart to tell him I'd been planning such a project for some time; in any case, a partnership of some kind seemed safer than letting him write the book without me!

In the actual preparation of the lines, I am indebted to many who over the years have offered advice, gentle criticism and encouragement, in particular my friend and Mikado colleague of many years' standing, Richard Angas. Blessed with only having to appear in the second act – but nonetheless having to be in the theatre by curtain up – he has been a regular and essential test-audience for my latest additions to the Little List. The joy of hearing his laugh and subsequent approval is vital – as is his silence when I offer him something about which he has no clue whatsoever (he is, by his own admission, an erratic reader of newspapers, and certainly would not stoop to digging around for some of the more scurrilous things I find). We frequently joke about the dressing room status afforded him: he used to get No. 3 at the Coliseum, but had to be demoted when, after refurbishment, the room mysteriously became smaller (and he remained very big). He is now to be found in dressing room No. 6, opposite the gents loos that are often blocked. Only in Venice did he manage to make it to No. 1… but then the Italians always had a soft spot for title roles and benign dictators.

Finally, I would like to pay tribute to a dear friend and major contributor to this book, who sadly died during its preparation at the young age of 58. Kevin Chapple is responsible for many of the directions this book has taken. I first met him when he was theatre manager at the Savoy; the D'Oyly Carte was performing a season in 1989 and my third child was born shortly after I returned home one night from a performance of *The Mikado*. The following evening Kevin popped into my dressing room with a bottle of champagne – and that simple act of kindness began a friendship that saw him making trips to New York, Venice, and Holland among others to watch performances in which I was taking part. We would regularly meet for lunch. He was well-loved by all who came into contact with him, particularly performers and colleagues alike – he moved on to the Orange Tree Theatre in Richmond, and Opera Holland Park – his final post was at the Cadogan Hall. Kevin was a fount of information, with a wicked sense of humour, and a true interest in other people, many of whom will be reading this book. I am truly sorry that he was not able to see one of the fruits of our friendship.

PICTURE CREDITS

Photos: Bill Cooper: cover; Mary Evans Picture Library: 1;Billy Rafferty: 2, 6, 12, 13, 53, 100, 114, 113, 128, 133, 142, 147, 166, 182, 183; Jurjen Stekelenburg: 120, 121; David Warner Ellis: 13, 186; *Cartoons*: Sue Parmenter: 170; Olly Burton 75, 123, 137, 171; Nicholas Garland, by kind permission: 49; Solo Syndication on behalf of Daily Mail: 64 & 66; Mirrorpix on behalf of Daily Mirror: 50 and 78; Brighton Evening Argus: 54; Kathy Hayes Associates for David Levine, 88.

We are greatly indebted to the following collectors, who have kindly given permission for their material to be used: John Cannon: 54, 55, 77, 85, 98, 118, 134, 138, 159, 160; Peter Joslin: 15-28, 30, 40, 42, 185; Melvyn Tarran: 33, 34; Kevin Chapple: 10, 11, 35, 50, 56, 60, 64, 66, 67, 70, 83, 90, 93, 94, 102, 103, 107, 124, 126, 127; J. Donald Smith: 91, 92, 152; Ralph MacPhail Jnr. and the MacPhail Gilbert & Sullivan Collection: 149; Royal Academy of Music: 44-49

All other illustrations from the author's collection

First published 2008

by Pallas Athene (Publishers) Ltd
42 Spencer Rise, London NW5 1AP
www.pallasathene.co.uk

ISBN 978 1 84368 036 9

The publisher would particularly like to thank John Cannon, Peter Joslin, J. Donald Smith and Ralph MacPhail for their unstinting help, without which this book would not have been possible in its present form. Special thanks also to Iain Kerr of Goldberg and Solomon, whose songs are now available from iTunes

Cover picture: Richard Suart as Ko-Ko delivers the Little List
p 1 C. H. Workman as Ko-Ko
p 2 Richard Suart as Ko-Ko